Aspen Notebook: Cable and Continuing Education

Richard Adler
Walter S. Baer

Aspen Workshop on
Uses of the Cable

Sponsored by the
Aspen Program on Communications
and Society

The Praeger Special Studies program—
utilizing the most modern and efficient book
production techniques and a selective
worldwide distribution network—makes
available to the academic, government, and
business communities significant, timely
research in U.S. and international economic, social, and political development.

Aspen Notebook:
Cable and
Continuing Education

PRAEGER SPECIAL STUDIES IN U.S. ECONOMIC, SOCIAL, AND POLITICAL ISSUES

Praeger Publishers   New York   Washington   London

Library of Congress Cataloging in Publication Data

Adler, Richard R.
  Aspen Notebook: Cable and Continuing Education

  (Praeger special studies in U.S. economic, social, and political issues)
  "Sponsored by the Aspen Program on Communications and Society."

  Bibliography: p. 175
  1. Television in education. 2. Community antenna television. 3. Evening
and continuation schools. I. Baer, Walter S., joint author. II. Aspen Program
on Communications and Society. II. Title.

  LC6574.A34   371.33 '58   73-14744

PRAEGER PUBLISHERS
111 Fourth Avenue, New York, N.Y. 10003, U.S.A.
5, Cromwell Place, London SW7, 2JL, England

Published in the United States of America in 1973
by Praeger Publishers, Inc.

© 1973 by the Aspen Program on Communications
and Society

Printed in the United States of America

Book composition by Curt Chelin, San Francisco

Preface

This volume is the first in a planned series of *Aspen Notebooks* on cable. Part I contains a report based on research carried out by the Aspen Workshop on Uses of the Cable. It describes the current status of continuing education, examines the history of the educational uses of television, then explores the prospects being created by the development of cable for extending access to continuing education. It also discusses in some detail a number of problems which will have to be resolved if such enterprises are to succeed. Each chapter is followed by remarks from participants in the Aspen Workshop Conference on the Cable and Continuing Education held at Aspen, Colorado, March 14-18, 1973. A final chapter summarizes the proposals arising from that conference and features nine recommendations for local and national initiatives regarding the implementation of cable in continuing education.

Part II of the book contains additional source and reference materials for those wanting more information on the subjects raised in Part I. It includes descriptions of three television-supported educational programs (the first well-established, the second new and the third hypothetical); an explanation by James Gibbons of the criteria for successful educational uses of television; several abstracts of related reports and studies; a brief glossary of terms used in this book; and an annotated bibliography.

The authors would like to express their thanks to the following for the parts they played in the preparation of this volume: The National Endowment for the Humanities, the John and Mary R. Markle Foundation, and the Aspen Program on Communications and Society for their support for the Workshop on Uses of the Cable; Robert Hind of the Academy for Educational Development, who helped write the original paper which formed the basis for Part I of the *Notebook;* William Rivers and Frank Newman of Stanford University, who reviewed the manuscript; Maria   Savage, who prepared the abstracts and bibliography; Diane Willis, Susan Sanders, Rich Kuhn, and Jim Arntz for their editorial assistance in preparing the manuscript for publication; the many people, both in education and the cable industry, who shared their experiences and ideas with us through interviews. And finally, special thanks to all the participants in the Workshop Conference on the Cable and Continuing Education, whose statements and comments form an important element of this book.

Palo Alto, California   Richard Adler
                                                        Walter S. Baer

Participants in the
Workshop Conference on The Cable and Continuing Education

Aspen, Colorado — March 14-18, 1973

DOUGLASS CATER
Director, Aspen Program on
Communications and Society

FORREST CHISMAN
Executive Assistant,
The John and Mary R.
Markle Foundation

GENEVIEVE CORY
Canada College
Redwood City, California

W. BOWMAN CUTTER
Director, Cable Television
Information Center

ROBERT T. FILEP
Associate Commissioner
for Educational Technology,
U.S. Office of Education

W. TODD FURNISS
Director, Commission on
Academic Affairs, American
Council on Education

JAMES GIBBONS
Stanford University;
Newman Commission on
Higher Education

SAMUEL GOULD
Institute for Educational
Development;
Chairman, Commission on
Non-Traditional Study

JESSIE HARTLINE
Dean, University College;
Director, Open University at
Rutgers University

DAVID HILL
Ohio Board of Regents

AMOS B. HOSTETTER, JR.
Executive Vice-President,
Continental Cablevision

CYRIL O. HOULE
Professor of Education,
University of Chicago;
Commission on
Non-Traditional Study

ARMAND L. HUNTER
Director, Continuing Education
Service, Michigan State
University

THOMAS JAMES
President, Spencer Foundation

CHARLOTTE JONES
Director, Community Programming,
Teleprompter Corporation

GERALD LESSER
Harvard School of Education;
Board of Advisors, Children's
Television Workshop

JACK McBRIDE
Director, State University
of Nebraska

MICHAEL McCRUDDEN
American Television and
Communications Corporation

SIG MICKELSON
Professor of Journalism,
Northwestern University

JAMES MILLER
Vice President, Academy for
Educational Development

SHAFEEK NADER
American Association of
Community Colleges

FRANK NORWOOD
Executive Secretary, Joint
Council on Educational
Telecommunications

Participants in the
Workshop Conference on The Cable and Continuing Education

JAY RAEBEN
President, Visual Information
Systems

JOHN SCHONLEBER
National Endowment for the
Humanities

JOSEPH SLATER
President, Aspen Institute
for Humanistic Studies

STUART SUCHERMAN
The Ford Foundation

NORMAN WATSON
Chancellor, Coast Community
College District,
Orange County, California

BARRY ZORTHIAN
President, Time-Life Cable

FRANK DOBYNS
ARCA Foundation

Contents

PART I

Contents

PART II

Foreword

by Douglass Cater

Mankind has been singularly unskilled in promoting the uses of new technology for large social purposes. This was the starting premise for our effort to study possible convergence points of cable television and continuing education in America. Of only two facts we felt certain: first, that the cable has the capacity for vast expansion of our channels of communication; second, that there will be a vastly expanded need for education beyond the classroom in the years ahead.

In examining the possibilities offered by technology's potential and education's need, one might be inclined to rely on the free workings of the marketplace. But the marketplace for such an enterprise will be anything but free; the cable will find its way into the homes and educational institutions of America only according to rules and regulations laid down by governmental authority. Nor is continuing education, like other forms of schooling, likely to get very far without substantial public subsidy. A policy of *laissez faire* is not one of our options. Choices must be made. Experiments must be tried. A strategy must be shaped.

Looking ahead, one prophet has predicted that the coming communications revolution will change life styles as radically as did the motor car earlier in the century. There is also a dark side to this future. Just as the automobile turned us into nomads of the road, so the new communications could make us nomads of the home, wandering desultorily among its myriad offerings. We face the prospect of opening vaster wastelands rather than exploring new frontiers of information, entertainment and enlightenment.

The *Aspen Notebook: Cable and Continuing Education* is another product of the continuing effort by the Aspen Program on Communications and Society to sponsor studies, conduct seminars and workshops and disseminate findings that will identify public choices of critical importance in shaping our communications future. The Aspen Program is attempting to build a wider community of those prepared to take a serious and disciplined interest in communications policy. Our mission, in brief, is to invent an alternative to the Orwellian vision of 1984.

PART I

Introduction

The entrepreneurs who first developed cable television gave little thought to educational applications. They were bent on furnishing better TV reception to subscribers who could not receive clear pictures off the air. They still are. Improved reception is still the economic basis for cable television in the cities, towns and rural areas where it has prospered over the past 20 years. But cable now has far more to offer than sharper pictures of Walter Cronkite or Shea Stadium. As cable begins entering our major urban centers, new forces are at work which raise great expectations for cable as a provider of public services and as an agent of social change. Among the new developments:

- Cable technology can now supply dozens of channels, many more than are needed for conventional broadcast signals. It can select or restrict viewing audiences—for pay-TV events, for example, or medical seminars. It offers the prospect of two-way interaction between viewers and the program source.
- Since off-the-air television reception is already good in most urban centers, cable systems are able to win subscribers only by offering more services than the mere re-transmission of broadcast television.
- New federal regulations require expanded technical capacities and special channels for public service applications.
- More and more people are becoming aware of cable's potential for greater program diversity and for increased accessibility of information and improved communications in their neighborhoods and cities.

Of all public services on cable, education usually is singled out as the most promising. A lavish assortment of applications have been proposed: elementary and secondary classroom instruction, college and university degree courses, on-the-job training, specialized education for the handicapped and the gifted, for slow learners, prisoners, professionals and the unemployed. A recent report on cable television and education by the National Cable Television Association describes cablecast educational programming for almost every segment of society from "The Wired Sandbox" to "The Senior Scene." Recognizing this potential, the Federal Communications Commission has mandated one free educational access channel on all new cable systems built in major metropolitan areas.

But there is no guarantee that the potential will be fully realized. Cable television is the latest in a train of twentieth-century technical developments, including radio, films, audio tapes, broadcast television and computer-assisted instruction that were also supposed to bring about revolutions in educational quality and productivity. They failed to do so, and hundreds of books and articles have documented their failures. Will cable television be any different? How can it avoid becoming another "solution looking for problems"? In what ways can cable and related developments in communications serve the nation's educational needs?

The Aspen Workshop on the Cable asked a distinguished group of educators, cable executives and others concerned with the humanistic uses of communications technology to consider these questions at a conference held in Aspen, Colorado, in March 1973. The conference focused on cable television and continuing education, or non-traditional study, for two reasons: (1) Recent years have seen a growing recognition of the need to extend formal learning beyond campus boundaries to people who are not well-served by the existing educational system. (2) Institutions for non-traditional study are generally newer, faster growing and more flexible than their traditional counterparts. Consequently, they may be readier to take up such technological innovations as cable television.

The Aspen Workshop on the Cable saw both short-term and long-range benefits in bringing together policy-makers and practitioners from the cable television and continuing education communities. The first objective was to discuss existing programs and proposals and to make specific program and policy recommendations. A few success stories carry far more conviction than whole volumes of visionary rhetoric. Existing educational institutions have clear opportunities to begin pilot projects with presently operating cable systems, but as the following chapters make clear, a number of barriers must be surmounted to accomplish this.

A second objective was to outline more clearly the longer-term implications of cable and related communications technology for continuing education, in light of the rapid evolution in both areas. All of us tend to view a new technical advance in terms of the marginal improvements in present-day practices that it makes possible. Still, the greatest impact will likely come from wholly new uses. Computers, after all, were developed in the 1940s principally to make gunnery tables more accurate. Our present visions for the uses of cable television in education may be equally myopic.

Finally, the Aspen Workshop hoped to strengthen the dialogue between leaders in cable television and continuing education. The confluence of these two communities demands planning and cooperation at both the national and local levels. New policies and strategies must be developed. Many groups not previously concerned with television—educators and investment bankers, local officials and academic scholars—must contribute their knowledge and skills to the development of this new medium. Only then can we hope to realize the potential of the cable in facilitating the ideal of lifelong learning.

The Rise of Continuing Education

1

Specialized education for adults has been with us in various forms since the founding of this nation. But the idea of providing a wide range of organized educational opportunities to adult Americans is a relatively new concept. Sponsoring institutions today range from employers and government agencies to conventional schools—secondary, post-secondary, and proprietary (privately owned and operated); and the content of their programs may be academic, strictly job-related, or directed primarily to the personal needs and interests of the students. The scope of these programs varies from short-term courses, seminars and lecture series to ambitious learning programs more intensive than those in conventional schools.

Information on the current magnitude of continuing education is confusing and often conflicting, primarily because there is little agreement on what programs to include in compiling such data. Figures on participation in continuing education are not even reported in the usual summaries of educational statistics. The largest survey of continuing education, which was conducted nearly a decade ago, revealed that approximately 25 million adult Americans—nearly one out of five—had been active in one or another form of learning during the previous year.* Nearly 50 percent of those interviewed said that they had taken at

*John W.C. Johnstone and Ramon J. Rivera, *Volunteers for Learning: A Study of the Educational Pursuits of American Adults.* Chicago: Aldine Publishing Company, 1965, pp. 1-2.

least one educational course since leaving school.

More recent evidence suggests that the growth of continuing education has accelerated in the past decade. Stanley Moses of the Education Policy Research Center at Syracuse University has developed estimates and projections of adult enrollments which suggest the magnitude of this growth. He concludes that over 60 million adults participated in such programs in 1970 and that the number would grow to over 82 million by 1975.* Table 1, reprinted here from the Moses study, traces this growth according to the type of sponsoring institution or program.

Table 1. Growth of Various Continuing Education Programs

Type of Institution or Program	Millions Enrolled†						
	1940	1950	1955	1960	1965	1970	1975 (projected)
Organizational programs –business, government, military	8.2	10.2	10.9	13.0	14.5	21.7	27.4
Proprietary schools	2.5	3.5	3.5	4.0	7.8	9.6	18.1
Anti-poverty programs	–	–	–	–	2.8	5.1	7.0
Correspondence courses	2.7	3.4	3.5	4.5	5.0	5.7	6.7
TV-based instruction	–	–	–	.01	5.0	7.5	10.0
Other adult programs in colleges, high schools, libraries, social organizations, etc.	3.9	4.8	5.1	6.6	9.1	10.7	13.2
	17.3	21.9	23.0	28.3	44.2	60.3	82.4

By comparison with the Moses figures, the total 1970 enrollment in all conventional institutions from kindergarten through graduate levels was just under 60 million. It must be acknowledged, of course, that conventional institutions generally demand much more of a learner's time, and that it is more difficult to avoid double-counting of participants in adult programs. Clearly, however, continuing education is large and growing.

This growth in the adult demand for more education is not so much the result of the success of our educational institutions in instilling a yearning for life-long learning, although that is a frequently stated goal of these institutions. Rather

---

*Stanley Moses, *The Learning Force: A More Comprehensive Framework for Educational Policy.* Syracuse University, Publications in Continuing Education, Occasional Papers No. 25, October 1971, p. 19.

†Note that these figures represent only those persons engaged in formal educational programs and not those benefiting from the more passive educative opportunities, such as cultural events, documentaries and lectures.

adult education has grown primarily as a result of certain fundamental changes in our society, including:

- a rapidly changing technology which requires constant upgrading of employment skills or preparation for new careers;
- a shift from the older ethic of sticking to a single career or job to an acceptance and even an expectation of changes in one's occupation;
- a technology and social climate which allow increased leisure time for all occupations, including homemakers;
- an increasingly higher educational level in the population, which in turn promotes further education.

These changes have taken place at a rate that has outstripped the ability of educational institutions to respond to them. A formal education which ends at age 20 or 25 and which takes place almost entirely within the confines of a classroom or campus can no longer be considered an adequate preparation for a lifetime of fulfilling work and personal pursuits.

The problems brought about by this discrepancy are well-described in the *Report on Higher Education* issued in 1971 by the Newman Commission (named after its chairman, Frank Newman of Stanford University). The *Report* argues that American post-secondary education is currently organized around two fundamental paths of study—academic and vocational—and that the limiations of both approaches are becoming increasingly acute. For example, in a society in which 50 percent of high school graduates now go directly on to college, the simple fact of college attendance is no longer a guarantee of employability. The possession of a liberal arts degree is often useful only as a means of entry into more specialized graduate study. Yet large numbers of undergraduates undertake such courses of study simply because it seems to be the proper thing to do and because the alternatives to attending college seem even less attractive.

Nor are programs of vocational education much more useful or satisfactory. These programs are usually limited, in reputation and in fact, to training for semi-skilled or blue-collar occupations rather than for the growing number of highly skilled technical jobs. Moreover, the courses of study offered frequently bear little relation to the actual supply and demand in the job marketplace. Finally, such narrowly focused vocational training programs, however effective, run the increasing risk of providing skills that are marketable today but obsolete tomorrow.

The Newman Commission argues that we need to develop an educational system which recognizes that

> *people mature at different ages and arrive at the point of wanting to learn by different routes. Some 18-year-olds are simply not ready for any further education, and some for whom a conventional college education would be suitable are more ready at age 30. Others with job experience, either before or during or after undergraduate training, are ready for education that may*

be broader ranging or may be more specific and technical than the conventional. *

Unfortunately, our educational system still suffers from what the commission vividly describes as "educational apartheid"—the widely shared belief that "young people ought to be engaged in higher education from about 18 . . . [and] that older students should be seen as atypical." The great irony is that if Stanley Moses' statistics are correct, these "atypical" students now make up a majority of those engaged in formal study. The Newman Commission's *Report* is an eloquent call for recognition of the needs of these adult students.

Many of the Newman Commission findings are reaffirmed by the recent two-year study of the Commission on Non-Traditional Study, under grants from the Carnegie Corporation and the Educational Foundation of America. The commission identifies a number of praiseworthy new programs of non-conventional study, and the general tone of its report † is more optimistic than that of the Newman Commission. However, it too calls for (1) substantial increases in support for new programs of non-traditional study, (2) the re-orientation of educational institutions to give the needs of the learner highest priority, and (3) the creation of new mechanisms and institutions to make access to continuing education possible for all those who want it.

Who are these non-traditional students and what do they want to study? They are, above all, students who are seeking out further education but are not available for full-time, conventional on-campus programs and therefore need educational services at times and places convenient to them. They are usually but not necessarily older than the conventional "student age" of 18-24. Almost all of them bear responsibilities of jobs and families to which their educational needs must be subordinated, even though their educational interests are often great.

Their educational interests are also enormously varied. One convenient subdivision is between those seeking credit toward a specific degree or certificate and those who seek learning for more immediate purposes. In the credit area, for example, there are those who dropped out of high school and subsequently find that they need to acquire a diploma or equivalency in order to be suitably employed. A Corporation for Public Broadcasting project found that 8.1 million Americans aged 25 to 44 attended but did not complete high school. There are also the high school graduates who attended but never completed college and are now seeking a part-time course of study ranging from occupational programs to pre-professional and professional training to B.A. and B.S. degrees. In this regard, the Newman Commission has reported that of the more than 1 million

---

*Frank Newman *et al., Report on Higher Education.* Washington: Government Printing Office, 1971, p. 8.

†*Diversity by Design* (an abstract of the major findings and recommendations in the Commission on Non-Traditional Study's forthcoming final report), February 2, 1973.

entering college each year, fewer than half complete two years of study and only about one-third ever complete a four-year course of study.

Among the "non-credit" clients for continuing education, there are many who seek short-term professional or occupational upgrading or updating. These range from the physician who wants to keep up to the farmer who seeks crop advice. Some may be motivated by a desire to be more productive or effective; others may need to meet basic licensure requirements.* Still other non-credit students may simply want to enrich their lives through the guidance of an instructor and an educational experience. Among the latter are those seeking to master the skills of chosen hobbies or pastimes; those striving for broad intellectual growth, such as the thousands who have availed themselves of Great Books and current affairs programs; and those who seek practical information to help cope with problems of a complex society. This last category includes persons who wish to be better informed consumers, who need help in health care and child rearing, who are functionally illiterate or lack other basic skills, and who need advice in such matters as family finance and budgeting, computing income taxes, and dealing with the ever-increasing demands of governmental programs and regulations.

Some idea of the numbers of people who express interest in various kinds and fields of continuing education are indicated in Table 2, which gives the results from a national survey made for the Commission on Non-Traditional Study. The same range of interests and emphasis on vocational study were also found in similar interview surveys conducted in 1972 in rural northeast California and in representative locations in Colorado.†

These varied interests illustrate the wide range of demands that are being placed on the educational system. They also suggest the wide variety of people and motives that must be accommodated. Learners in these diverse categories will have different levels of commitment and motivation—some must be lured, others simply accepted. In addition, they will have different levels of sophistication and preparation and different financial circumstances and attitudes— some will gladly pay, others can or will not. There is evidence that those who have the greatest need for further education are the least likely to get it.†† The

---

*A growing number of professions are requiring periodic course work leading to re-certification and/or examination by review boards established by governmental or professional bodies. For example, the California Department of Consumer Affairs estimates that in California today 250,000 professionals and para-professionals are required by law to pursue continuing education, up from virtually zero two years ago. The number is expected to grow to about a million by the end of the decade.

†These surveys were for projects of the California Coordinating Council for Higher Education and the Colorado Commission on Higher Education.

††In attempting to identify and estimate the numbers and characteristics of potential continuing students, educators are handicapped by this divergence between identified need and actual demand. We can pinpoint with some accuracy the size of particular need groups, such as young adult non-graduates of high school, and some efforts have been

Table 2. What Adults Would Like To Study*

	Total choices†	First choice†
Vocational subjects (architecture, business skills, commercial art, computer science, cosmetology, education and teacher training, engineering, industrial trades, journalism, law, management skills, medicine and dentistry, nursing, salesmanship, technical skills)	78.2%	43.0%
Hobbies and recreation (crafts, fine and visual arts, flight training, performing arts, safety, sports and games, travel and living in foreign countries)	62.8%	13.4%
Home and family life (child development, gardening and flower arranging, home repairs, sewing and cooking).	56.0%	12.0%
Personal development (investment, occult sciences, personal psychology, physical fitness and self-development, public speaking) . . .	54.3%	6.8%
General education (basic education, biological sciences, creative writing, English-language training, Great Books, humanities, languages, physical sciences, social sciences)	47.9%	12.6%
Public affairs (citizenship, community problems and organizations, consumer education, environmental studies, public affairs).	36.3%	4.5%
Religious studies	15.4%	3.0%
Agriculture and farming	10.9%	2.9%

made to determine interests, as illustrated by the data developed for the Commission on Non-Traditional Study. However, there is little information to establish more precise correlations among need, interest and participation of continuing education students. A suggested pilot project described in Part II, p. 149, is intended to remedy this problem at least in part.

*Reprinted from *Diversity by Design* (see previous footnote, p. 10)

†Percent of adults not engaged in full-time study who say they would like to learn more about the subjects.

Johnstone and Rivera study of adult students indicates that participation in continuing education is strongly linked to income, occupation and past education. Their data shows that a college graduate working in a white-collar occupation is about six times more likely to engage in further learning than a blue-collar worker who has never gone beyond grade school.*

These differences between learners' requirements and motivational levels among adult students call for some individualization of instruction—at least to the extent of course offerings to narrow and specialized audiences. And this is where cable television comes in, with its ability to direct its content efficiently and economically to even a handful of learners. Programs that can count on broad general enrollments can and should rely on broadcast television and on other methods. Those that are directed to smaller numbers, or that must divide a class into small groups to provide essential interaction, are the special targets of cable. And in these situations, cable may be the best hope for expanding access to continuing education.

*Johnstone and Rivera, p. 7 (see previous footnote, p. 7)

Discussion

Samuel B. Gould

Dr. Gould is president of the Institute for Educational Development and director of the Aspen Institute's Program on Education for a Changing Society
(APEX). For the past two years he has also served as chairman of the Commission on Non-Traditional Study, which was established with support from the
Carnegie Corporation to explore "the need for, the nature of and the potential
for non-traditional education in this country." Dr. Gould reported to the Aspen
Workshop conference on the results of the commission's research and its major
recommendations. Of particular interest was the following statement regarding
the commission's conclusions about the need for new educational delivery systems, including cable, to reach the non-traditional student more effectively.

The Commission on Non-Traditional Study was a two-year effort, just concluded, that consisted of 26 leaders in education and related fields from all over
the country. Our commission was trying to assess the extent and the importance
of a movement in America toward the creation of a society that would offer
everyone a great diversity of educational opportunity. It was trying to emphasize the necessity for enduring high quality in every aspect of that movement.
It was trying to suggest specific actions—for a variety of educational, governmental or social institutions—that would assist in strengthening this concept of
educational opportunity and so come a little closer to the democratic ideal.

To achieve that purpose, the commission gathered data that indicated the
number of adults who say they want to keep on learning; the number who have
actually been learners during the past 12 months; and the number of institutions of higher learning today that are actually offering non-traditional programs (with the content of these programs). We also looked into what the obstacles are to those people who want to learn and what their attitudes are toward
traditional and non-traditional methods of study; the problems that these
people have in getting into non-traditional educational programs; the structural
forms of the courses and the instructional methods that are used; the measure-
ments of progress in non-traditional programs and the rewards that are offered
to the student; the assessment of institutions offering these programs; and the
financial implications of their adapting to these new ways of doing things.

We talked to literally hundreds of people all over the country in relatively
small groups. Some conversations had to do with educational technology;
some had to do with the problems of the community or junior college. Sometimes we found answers, and sometimes we just found that we needed to discover a great deal more than we knew at the present time. One of the areas,

for instance, in which we were never able to get answers that helped very much was in finance. All we discovered was that a lot of work needs to be done to find out whether non-traditional programs are more expensive or less expensive than traditional ones.

Our data revealed 79 million people who had reached the point where they had completed a high school education or its equivalent and wanted more education, yet had never had an opportunity to do anything about it or had not made that opportunity for themselves. We also found an enormous number—32 million—who had been involved over the past 12 months in evening classes, correspondence courses, extension courses, on-the-job training, private lessons, independent study, or television. Very little that we discovered in non-traditional studies was new, but we found that there were some 351 institutions involved in programs that you could call significantly non-traditional.

One of the things that always seemed to come up was the so-called definition that we ultimately came to for "non-traditional studies." Everyone kept saying, "Well, what *is* non-traditional study?" And it turned out to be virtually impossible to give them a definition. I don't know how many hours the commission spent discussing the matter. We had one member who simply dug his heels in and said, "If you aren't going to come up with a definition, I don't see any sense in doing this whole thing." And he said it from the first day we met until the last day we met. We finally concluded that non-traditional study is more an attitude than a system. Here is the tangential definition that we arrived at:

> *It is an attitude that puts the student first and the institutions second; concentrates more on the former's need than the latter's convenience; encourages diversity of individual opportunity; and de-emphasizes the time and space or even course requirements in favor of competence and, where applicable, performance. It is not a new attitude; it is simply a more prevalent one than before. It has concern for the learner of any age or circumstance, for the degree-aspirant or the person who finds a sufficient reward in enriching life through constant, periodic or occasional study. It is an attitude that can stimulate exciting and high quality educational progress; it can also, unless great care is taken to protect the freedom it offers, be the unwitting means to a lessening of academic rigor and even to charlatanism.*

One interesting sidelight to the commission report, which may have some significance for the things we talk about here, was that some of the people who said that they were tremendously interested and involved in non-traditional approaches to education are the most traditional in their own approaches as to how they want a problem solved. One of the major criticisms leveled against us when the report came out was that we didn't give specific answers that an institution could take and simply use on its campus. They said, "Where's your design for what we need to do?" This is exactly what we didn't want to do and what we would never have expected a non-traditional advocate to want us to do. We also discovered that the methods by which people—particularly over the age of 25—want to learn are inevitably the traditional methods. Something like 38 percent wanted to learn by the lecture method, and only 1 percent wanted to learn by television. Now that tells you something about what has to be done if we want to make education by cable television or any other kind of television really significant.

We based our specific recommendations around seven general areas. The first area has to do with life-long learning and the way in which it should be financed. Our commission recommended that we should work at the problem of providing financial aid to all post-secondary students. They would be able to draw on this money according to their educational needs, circumstances and continuing or recurrent interests. Now this is a very sweeping recommendation in what it implies for cost and for the whole future of education for the American people. Alan Pifer (president of the Carnegie Corporation) estimated that this would cost 22 billion dollars a year. That sounds like a lot of money until you begin to match it against some of the other expenditures that we make. Also, it isn't a question of whether we can afford to make that investment, but whether we can afford not to; because it will make an enormous difference in our economy as well as the general life of our people.

The interesting thing is that this is not a new idea. It is already being done in other countries—France, Germany and Great Britain have gone either all or part way in dong this. France is the most interesting illustration. In 1971 a law was passed which provided that .8 percent of the gross national product had to be set aside in a fund for the "worker" to be able to draw on for whatever educational purposes he thought were worthwile for himself, whether they had to do with vocation or with the general enrichment of his life and whether he took a sabbatical from his job for six months and went somewhere or whether he took week-end courses, special workshops or whatever. That .8 percent the first year, in 1972, amounted to 800 million dollars; and by 1975, that fund will have reached 2 billion dollars annually on which everybody can draw.

Germany has a similar scheme, and the United Kingdom and Sweden are moving in the same direction. So we're talking about something which is in being and for which we could find a formula just as other countries have. I think this is the most important recommendation which came out of the commission, although I don't think it was recognized as such. I say this with full realization that it will take years to get the American people and the American government to accept it and do something about it. But the time for talking about this and pushing for it is now. It won't take as long as some of us are fearful that it might.

Another area of recommendation was the obsession for degree-earning which has swept our country and which the commission thinks ought to be off-set by getting the colleges and universities to think not so much about degree programs, but rather about the kinds of substantive courses and other materials which they present and which the student can choose from. Then, if the student wants to get a degree, fine; if he doesn't, he still is doing a worthwhile thing. The fact that everybody thinks he needs to be working toward a degree is most unfortunate. I don't have any illusions about how quickly one can make the colleges and universities change in this respect. However, some are beginning to think in these terms and I believe more will.

Another very important area of recommendation, one that will have direct connection with cable television, is the re-direction of faculty understanding and commitments toward new technological developments in education and a more intelligent and widespread use of this technology. We emphasized programming for cable television, knowledge of computers, the possibility of satellite broadcasting, and the use of video-tape recorders and audio cassettes. There is a need for tremendous numbers of workshop programs all over the country to get faculty to understand these new approaches and opportunities and to show them how it is possible to use them. This is really very easy in many instances; the technological aspects are not as frightening as some faculty seem to think they are.

Another area, which I won't dwell on here, is the need to create certain new kinds of agencies in order to deal with the non-traditional programs. The external degree [a degree program with limited or no on-campus residence requirement] has created all kinds of necessities that didn't exist before: How does a student have his credits evaluated? Where does he go? Suppose he lives in California and moves to the East Coast. Where does he get his credits put together if he wants some kind of external degree? There has to be some kind of agency to deal with this.

A related area, and one of the most important of all, is that of creating new evaluative tools by which to measure non-traditional results. If you are going to talk, for example, about work experience as an educational factor and give credit toward a degree, how do you measure that work experience educatively? I think this is the Achilles heel of the whole non-traditional movement. We are accused of being willing to give credit for just about anything, and if we continue down that path, we are going to destroy the possibilities of a very wonderful movement. The opportunity for the individual to move in the educational path that he chooses for himself with the right kind of advice and counsel is really marvelous, but it must not become nothing more than the granting of all kinds of educational rewards for experiences that don't mean anything. Therefore, the commission has recommended that we get started right away on developing effective evaluative tools for non-traditional study.

The remaining two areas of recommendation by the commission have to do with the collaboration and coordination between the formal educational system and all the alternate systems that have been developing for so long around the country. I won't go into the specifics, but these recommendations have to do with educational programs in business, industry, labor unions, and social agencies and in military establishments. I don't think we realize how many people get educated outside the formal system and how important those educational systems are.What we tried to do is set forth all these different systems and make some recommendations primarily indicating what had to be done. We couldn't really point to a lot that has been achieved in these areas and assure everybody that this is the way that it ought to be. We are not going to get to that point in non-traditional education for a long, long time, and I don't know that we ever should.

There were some things that we were quite frank to admit that we couldn't do at all. For instance, we never really got into the substantive elements of study itself. What kinds of courses would be non-traditional? What makes them different? For example, the external degree that is given in Great Britain by the Open University is one of the most traditional programs you ever saw, except that its presentation is non-traditional. Are there non-traditional subjects from an academic standpoint that need to be discovered or examined? In addition, the commission was never able to grapple with the basic concept of the kind of balance that ought to be present between the timely and the timeless in education. There are things we ought always to be examining, as well as the contemporaneous things that ought to be examined at the same time. How does a student get any sense of that balance?

Yet another unanswered matter concerned the relationship of work to the quality of life. We have created a society in which work has no relationship, in most instances, to the quality of a person's life. And now we've reached a point where the worker is realizing this and he wants a change. Well, here is a non-traditional area still to be explored.

Finally, we didn't even though the greatest enigma of all—the nature of the intellectual, emotional and social equipment that constitutes a modern, educated person. Is it different from what it was 100 years ago? A thousand years ago? A tremendous amount of work needs to be done to find the answers to all these questions.

Discussion

Armand L. Hunter

Dr. Hunter is professor and director of the Continuing Education Service at Michigan State University and immediate past president of the National University Extension Association. He described to the conference the response of continuing education professionals to the new visibility and prestige of the field.

Continuing education represents a kind of educational paradox; because while we have a new status in the field, we also have new problems. The *troika* of teaching, research and public service, which has been the framework of the educational process since time immemorial, has always placed public service, which includes continuing education, at the lower end of the priority scale. Now all of a sudden, we find a tremendously increased interest in life-long education. All of a sudden, we're moving up in priority. This change is being reflected in reports from numerous commissions, task forces and committees sponsored by governments, foundations and institutional interests which have been established in the past few years. All of these studies put extension or continuing education in a new priority relationship and indicate a new field of interest in the educational establishment.

This higher priority comes about primarily through recognition on the part of faculty and administrators that education is a life-long process; it is no longer something that is conducted for the 18- to 22-year-old and chopped up in certain chronological segments related to types of degrees. Educators are also recognizing that the student body is changing. The students are not necessarily coming now and registering as freshmen, staying for four years and then leaving with a baccalaureate degree, or staying on for a year or so more and getting a masters degree. They're coming in, staying a short time, dropping out, re-entering, etc.

There is also recognition of the need for institutions to provide a broader base of educational resources and support to keep up with an ever-expanding range of educational needs and demands from the community. Public demand upon educational institutions as primary resources is increasing. Out of this is coming a new interest and a new concern with the process of continuing education and its place within the context of the institutional educational system. The ivory tower, I think I can safely say, is now becoming a little bit more of an open court.

On the other hand, continuing education is in trouble in terms of deciding which divisions of the university will be given the responsibility for making the institution's resources available to the adult and the general public. The educational establishment views the professionals in the field—the continuing education faculty, staff and administrators—as a priesthood whose religion consists primarily of its methodologies. This is because the structuring of extension divisions is primarily defined by independent study, conferences and institutes, community development, broadcasting and other types of delivery systems—which are mostly unfamiliar to the regular faculty. The professional design of the continuing education system is in trouble, because the educational establishment really believes that the professionals are incapable of developing the proper "metaphysics" of life-long education and, therefore, that the establishment must take over. The new religion, in other words, is too important to be left to this professional priesthood. Thus, we are seeing a much greater interest in continuing education at higher institutional levels, as represented by the American Council on Education, the Commission on Non-Traditional Study and so forth. Not too many of the people who are involved in these commissions and studies, however, are the practical operators, the professional people in the field.

Now, just what is taking place? We know there is a decrease in full-time residential students, and the statistics imply that this decrease is going to continue. We also know that there is a move in a number of institutions today to develop budgeting that is based upon the Program Budgeting System, in whch the production of student credit hours is the measure of educational support. When you have this taking place, the colleges and the departments are suddenly forced to develop a measure of accountability and productivity; for the production of student credit hours and the number of "full-time equivalent students" that they can show become the determinants of their annual operating budgets. Thus, all of a sudden, the adult, the non-traditional, the part-time students who were left to the extension and the public service divisions of the university have become important. Why? Because they produce student credit hours which can be translated into this full-time equivalency.

In other words, the traditional academic units and administrators have seen the light here. They are now beginning to move to take over this particular program as a part of the regular on-going, traditional functions of the academic units. If you project this pattern and this development, eventually the continuing education division as a separate identifiable unit will disappear. It will become a function and a responsibility, then, of the departments, the disciplines within the colleges and of the university as a whole. You will no longer have a continuing education division; you will have a continuing education university.

From the standpoint of the educational system and the educational process, this is all right. But from the standpoint of the professional administrators and practitioners in the field, this represents problems. Let me give you some examples. Number one: The March 12, 1973, edition of the *Chronicle of Higher Education* has an article which says "CLEP draws the fire of the English professors." CLEP [College Level Examination Program] is recognized as an innovative attempt to measure student achievement and accomplishment without having to go through a long traditional learning process. This threatens professors' jobs, which is where the bind is beginning to really get tight. Number two: California's four-year college and university systems are fighting a plan to establish a statewide off-campus university. Number three: The University of Illinois is challenging the need to establish a new "university without walls" to be called Lincoln State University. But as I said, this is really not all bad; and I don't think the paradox is a real one. If we could move the total resources of the university into a position where they can respond more effectively to the educational demands and needs that exist in our society, this would be to the good.

The same observations apply to educational media and communications technology. For many, many years educational broadcasters and those involved in instructional technology have suffered from the same "marginal-man syndrome" —the same problem of relating effectively to the educational resources of the total institution. If you do something about moving them to a higher priority level, then they also will have a more effective involvement in the total institution and in the production of broadcast educational materials that could be effectively utilized through the delivery systems that are in existence. On the other hand, there will always be a need for some direct administrative control of the delivery systems, because obviously the faculty are not going to be able to run a broadcasting station or a cable channel or a conference center.

In conclusion, perhaps the observation of T.S. Eliot would sum us up more than anything else. "Between the idea and the reality, between the motion and the act, falls the shadow." The present state of continuing education and CATV or broadcast education seems increasingly bright and the future even brighter. But in many respects, I believe both are in a period of change and shadow. Between the rhetoric of our idea and its reality, between the motion to implement and the act of fulfillment, come all the present difficulties of realization.

Television and Education

2

Television is generally accepted today as a legitimate part of the American education system, especially as an aid to in-school instruction. Nearly 50 percent of all elementary school classrooms are now equippped with television sets, and during the academic year, over 40 percent of the broadcast hours of the country's public television stations are devoted to instructional programming for in-school use. In 1970, these stations produced and televised over 17,000 hours of instructional programs, accounting for approximately one-fourth ($25 million) of the revenues received by all PTV stations. Overall, the National Association for Educational Broadcasters estimates that some 15 million students in the United States utilize television as part of their formal education.

While most instructional television has been on the elementary and secondary level, a number of successful uses of telecommunications have been made at the college level as well. Colorado State University, for example, offers a number of courses relying heavily on television, primarily in the "skills" area. An accounting course has produced student learning above the national average, as measured by standardized tests; and in the area of medical education, a televised course is used for most of the instruction in anatomy with good results. Portland Community College is one of a number of community colleges which have established "learning centers" where students have access to a wide range of learning equipment—"live" tutoring, computer-based instruction and audio and video cassettes. To date, such programs tend to be isolated to single campuses, with little sharing or interchange. Most television clearinghouses and distribution activities are still limited to the pre-college level.

Sufficient evidence has been gathered over the past years to confirm students can, in general, learn as effectively from television as from face-to-face instruction. Available research also indicates that "there is no general area where TV cannot be used efficiently to teach students."* Despite this evidence, the amount of time a typical student spends learning from television in school remains small, and the figure declines as he progresses through the grades. Why? A major reason is that the effective use of television is an enterprise demanding considerable skill and experience both in the production of programming and in its use at the receiving end. But while a great deal of money has been invested in the construction of ITV facilities and the purchase of equipment, no corresponding investment has been made in the production and implementation of educational programs.

Few schools have made significant commitments to integrating televised instruction into their curricula (the Hagerstown, Maryland, public schools are an often-cited exception). As a result, the public's multi-billion dollar investment† in educational technology has not paid off well, and ITV remains a peripheral element in the educational system. Television's promise to upgrade the quality of classroom instruction, broaden the curriculum and provide opportunities for accelerated learning has been largely unfulfilled.

Contemplating the disappointing record of the use of instructional media in the schools, James Coleman offered the following observation on the relations between education and the developing communications technologies:

> *The communication structure of society can affect education in two quite different ways. One is through application of new communications technology in schools: the use of closed-circuit television, computer consoles in the classroom, visual-aid equipment, and a wide range of other new possibilities. Some of these applications, potential and actual, promise to create sharp changes in the schools. It is these effects on education that technological changes in communication ordinarily bring to mind. But it has been characteristic of these applications that their promise precedes their reality by some years and that when the reality comes it never quite seems to match the expectation.*
>
> *The second kind of effect that the communication structure of society has on education is very different. It is through changes in communication structure* outside *educational institutions, powerful and pervasive changes that have unplanned and unanticipated effects on schools. These effects are often not recognized until after they have wrought their changes. The reality pre-*

---

*Godwin S. Chu and Wilbur Schramm, *Learning from Television: What the Research Says.* Washington: National Association of Educational Broadcasters, 1967.

†James Gibbons reports that Michael Annison and Lawrence Grayson of the U.S. Office of Education give a figure of $3 billion as their estimate of the federal investment in instructional technology from 1960 to 1970.

cedes the promise and is more powerful than the expectation.

These indirect effects are by-products of technological change in the communication structure of society. As such, one might expect them to be less important than the effects of direct, planned introduction of new communication technology in education. This, I believe, is not so today. The indirect impact of changes in the communication structure of society has been and will be so great that the technological changes in the schools themselves must take place within the new frame that these developments create. *

If the history of instructional television over the past two decades illustrates Coleman's first effect, then the development of commercial television and cable surely are examples of the second effect. By facilitating a vast increase in the rate of information dissemination, they have helped accelerate the process of social and technological change, which has, in turn, contributed to the obsolescence of the traditional definitions of education—in particular, the concept that formal schooling ends at age 20 or 25. But if television is part of education's current problems, it may also be part of the solution as well.

The evidence presented in the previous chapter suggests that there are millions of adult Americans who are interested in and capable of learning. The evidence also suggests that the number of adults wishing to do so will continue to increase. Our concern is not in using television for the enrichment of existing school environments but in the possibilities for exploiting television's great reach to extend access to education beyond the classroom and campus. Augmented by cable, satellites and the video cassette, television has an important role to play in expanding the range and accessibility of continuing education, in general, and extramural education in particular.

While television can be a powerful educational tool, its value is totally dependent on the quality of the materials it transmits and the skill with which its use is implemented. An extremely useful set of guidelines for designing effective television-supported educational programs was recently developed by James Gibbons of Stanford University.† On the basis of his study of a number of educational programs here and abroad, he derived the following six criteria for successful educational applications of technology:

1. *The educational program must be planned for a specific target audience.*
2. *Specific educational objectives that are relevant to the needs and interests of the target audience must be clearly understood and agreed on.*
3. *A systematic multi-media approach must be used in which both knowledge*

---

*James Coleman, "Education in Modern Society," in Martin Greenberger, ed., *Computers, Communications, and the Public Interest.* Baltimore: John Hopkins University Press, 1971, p. 116.

†See Part II, p. 127, for the full text of Professor Gibbons criteria.

specialists and media specialists are employed.
4. *Educators who are capable of learning and understanding the instructional characteristics of various media must be found.*
5. *Clear and careful provision for personal interaction . . . must be made.*
6. *Evaluation and feedback arrangements must be made to monitor audience reaction and change the instructional material to suit audience needs.*

Professor Gibbons also notes that in the successful programs, technology plays an important but usually not a dominant role. In other words, technology is just one component in a systematic approach to the delivery of education either on or off campus.

The outstanding accomplishments of two innovative projects—"Sesame Street" in the U.S. and the Open University in England—have helped stimulate interest in the use of television for extramural education. The measurable success of these two projects has convincingly demonstrated the practical as well as the theoretical ability of television to provide effective, high-quality education. Not surprisingly, these programs are receiving wide distribution. "Sesame Street" is being shown in many foreign countries, and four American universities are experimenting at present with the use of Open University course materials under a grant from the Carnegie Corporation.

A key element in the success of both enterprises has been that they are directed at meeting needs which would have been difficult or impossible to meet through the existing education system. "Sesame Street" is designed to provide basic linguistic and logic skills to 3- to 6-year-old pre-school children; the Open University is intended to provide a second chance to adults who were not able to attend college. In addition, it is clear that in both projects, television is used skillfully and with due regard for professional production standards. One of the most notable contributions of "Sesame Street" and the Open University has been the development of production teams in which the educator and the television producer are equal partners.

While these two projects are the most widely heralded new experiments in televised education, there are other programs in existence which are also successfully demonstrating the uses of television in providing extramural education:

1. The oldest on-going college-level program in the United States is Chicago's TV College. Since its inception in 1956, over 100,000 students have registered for its courses, and more than 75 percent of the registrants have completed the courses for credit. Studies comparing the performance of television students with on-campus students have shown that the television students do as well or better than the on-campus students. TV College courses are produced and televised by WTTW, Chicago's public television station. Fourteen of the TV College courses are currently available for national distribution through the Great Plains National ITV Library in Lincoln, Nebraska. The courses range from business writing and data processing to humanities and Shakespeare, from Afro-American history to educational psychology and public health science.

2. A group of 26 junior colleges in the Los Angeles area have joined together to form the Southern California Regional Consortium for Community College Television. Since 1967, the consortium has produced some half-dozen courses, with a current average enrollment of 5,000 students per year. It is currently offering two three-credit courses—history of art and introduction to astronomy—which are broadcast in the early morning over commercial television and repeated later in the day over the Los Angeles public television station. New course offerings are determined through discussions among the deans of instruction of the participating institutions, and the courses themselves are produced by individual colleges selected by the consortium board. Tutorial assistance, examinations, and credit are given by each school for students within its district. Although little systematic evaluation has been done by the consortium, preliminary studies of student performance indicate that television students perform about as well as students taking the same courses on-campus.

3. A number of higher education institutions are utilizing telecommunications to provide job-related and employer-financed courses for credit to engineers at their place of employment. These programs are distributed by videotape, or by direct transmission from campus to job site over special high-frequency channels. Although these programs have demonstrated that effective television learning can take place, even with advanced, highly technical subjects, they have not all met with economic success. Of the four programs studied by the authors, two have continued to prosper, one was shut down because of employer cutbacks, and another is in jeopardy, apparently for the same reason. This suggests that both employer and employee must see tangible benefits from the program if it is to receive continuing support. Evidence also suggests that the programs are more successful if scheduling is flexible enough to avoid conflicts with other employment responsibilities of the participating engineers.

Most of the educational programs we have been describing rely on broadcast television (usually through public television stations) to disseminate courses beyond the classroom and the campus. Projects like "Sesame Street" and, on a smaller scale, the Southern California TV Consortium have demonstrated the power of broadcast television to reach large audiences effectively, and this type of television will very likely remain the medium of choice for basic, general interest courses intended to appeal to the widest possible audiences. New projects are now underway at a number of institutions across the country to develop such courses, with considerable attention paid to sophisticated production techniques. For example, the Coast Community Colleges in Orange County, California, are producing a course on cultural anthropology which contains segments filmed in 30 countries around the world. Miami-Dade (Florida) Community College has produced a course on man and the environment which is based on a series of sophisticated documentary-type films on ecological concepts and issues.

These projects are obviously costly; the budget for the 30 half-hour segments of the cultural anthropology course is $500,000. In order to justify such costs, these courses must be disseminated and utilized on a wide scale, and at present, only broadcast television can provide this reach. However, the development of cable is creating a new delivery system capable of distributing a much wider range of specialized education to specific target audiences.

Discussion

Genevieve Cory

Dr. Cory is chairman of Consumer Education at Canada College, Redwood City, California. She received her doctorate from the University of California at Berkeley in the administration of higher education, with an emphasis on communications and instructional television. As the instructor for a televised consumer-education course for the past four years, Dr. Cory was well-qualified to describe for the Workshop conference the difficulties in learning the art of teaching via television.

With only a slight risk of overdramatizing, I could call my remarks "The Pitiful Plight of the Poor Practitioner." By recounting painful, self-inflicted bouts and the problems I encountered, I may be able to draw your attention to the problems of the practitioner and the teacher-producer. Although I run the risk of having my remarks seem critical, I will start out by saying that my programs have survived four years in spite of the educational system and not because of it. When educators point to the lack of use of television and its obvious failures, I am often tempted to say, "What did you expect, applying it as you did?"

The lack of understanding of technology has been a part of the problem. Lack of money has been a part of the problem. If you cannot break these bonds, you will dissipate even adequate funding and render the most remarkable educational tool since the textbook an inevitable failure.

For four years I have been the producer of the educational television series called "The Buying Game," which is delivered by open-circuit broadcasting to the San Francisco Bay Area and is sponsored by the Bay Area Consortium of Community Colleges. It is a course for college credit in a non-classroom format which I designed by hunch and intuition. I have also been coordinator for the Child Development Series which has taped two one-unit courses and plans a third. These three will constitute the first three units for credentialing of nursery school teachers in California.

My introduction into instructional television was very unexpected and excessively painful, which, I suspect, is fairly representative of the experience of most on-camera teachers. A brief review of a few of my aches and pains may help explain my title. In 1969 I was asked by telephone if I would teach a television course. I said no to myself 40 times and then finally accepted and immediately asked the television studio to send me some materials to prepare me for my job. They said, "What do you want?" There was nothing available for me. So I stumbled along and I suffered.

I had read McLuhan and I began to feel through my bones that this new medium was being badly served by rear-view mirror applications. I realized that we had on one side the educators, knowing nothing of television, and on the other the technicians, knowing nothing about education. And no one to close the gap. I, as an educator, felt a responsibility to deliver content. My director, as a technician, could not have cared less about content. He was concerned that I didn't make the show too complicated and that a camera didn't wiggle.

Another problem for me, as with any new on-camera teacher, was answering the question: "Who is that audience out there?" The red eye of the camera gives you no feedback. I think a lot of faculty resistance is based on this, but that resistance should be put in context. What the problem amounts to is this: If you try to teach more than 20 students in a classroom, you may just as well go to 200,000 or 2,000,000, because an instructor is kidding himself if he thinks he's reaching those students individually. Therefore, the argument about "individualized instruction" can be put aside as irrelevant in most cases. The real crux of the problem is that the instructor needs an audience more than the student needs a "live" lecturer; the average college teacher is a performer. That's a hard pill to take. Television is a serious threat since he needs that feedback to sustain him, and television's not going to give it to him.

I had to structure the program and I did it stumblingly. Fortunately, I had been trained to think visually, which is what many instructors in higher education have never learned. The 16 half-hour television shows that resulted were intentionally non-classroom in format. I think that, whether on cable or open broadcasting, a televised classroom format is suitable only for highly selected populations. We were serving independent students who could operate alone. Our main target groups were the disadvantaged and the minorities.

We built in listening groups with trained discussion leaders, and I reviewed enough research to know how to build in feedback. We did some research afterwards to find out who was out there and how they had reacted. We found out that the age distribution was almost even from 18 to 55-plus. The audience was two-thirds female and one-third male students. Their economic level was from welfare level through—and too heavily above—$15,000. We found that their educational background varied from graduate clear down through second-grade level.

We found that selective viewing was a very great hazard. When I did a whole show on automobile purchasing, if a viewer wasn't going to be purchasing an automobile that week, he turned off mentally since it just didn't seem useful. The second, third and fourth series were devised with 80 topics each, 5 on each show, to overcome these selective viewing problems. I brought in an expert for each topic and did interviews and demonstrations.

We identified the topics the viewers liked and thought they needed the most and found that the disadvantaged liked least the things they needed the most, such as credit, debt, garnishment, budgeting. They liked middle-class, "I'm-aspiring-to-buy" kinds of things. However, the viewers were really very accepting and forgiving of my very amateurish delivery when the content really had some meaning. They didn't really care that it was less than a very fine production.

I'd like to go on to some of the problems. The first was dealing with the administration—just getting and keeping the program going. I had to deal with three levels: the local college, the district, and the Bay Area TV Consortium. If a camel is a horse put together by a committee, only God in his infinite wisdom knows what a TV consortium is, because it is an incredibly unwieldy organization. I found, in working with the TV consortium, that I was surrounded by young administrators who had the powers of decision but no background whatsoever in television. It seems to be an unwritten law that young administrators can never admit what they don't know.

The technicians and the teachers had no vote over what was going to go on television. In the consortium meetings, the administrators would review curriculum proposals and ask questions like "Is it good television?" or "Are we serving community needs?" But when the vote came up, most of the votes went for the kind of solid academic lecture courses that are already listed in the catalogue of the least diversified college in the consortium. So there you have already doomed your most imaginative efforts.

Now, a great many of my problems arose because my program was successful. I found that the system was not geared to accept successful innovations. What is needed and is logical is what often cannot be done in an educational system. For example, I found no understanding among educators for the need for promotion to inform people that these courses were available. I found that because our program was so successful, because it generated so many telephone calls and so many new enrollments, that there wasn't an office girl in any department who would touch it. It was too much work. So to make it survive, I had to use student clerical help and take on the expense on myself. Even now, four years later, I am enrolling 1,500 students with two student clerical helpers. The courses have not yet been fully absorbed into the system.

A few other odd highlights: The computer would not spew out the enrollment forms nearly early enough to be useful. There was never enough lead time. The consortium dragged its heels so long that at one time I had to publish the student manual at my personal expense. I had to take a TB test to teach on television. Three counties insisted on holding my original teaching credentials in their hands at exactly the same time. I spent more time on this sort of thing than I did in developing two lessons.

Now I have a few suggestions: First, I would suggest for those who wish to develop better local programming that screening tests be developed for on-camera teachers. The present hit-and-miss method is much too costly in human and monetary terms. We must select teachers who have questioning attitudes, a jaundiced eye and a capacity and tolerance for experimentation. That will reduce the ranks rather terrifyingly fast. These teachers must be able to survive the searing experience of open exposure and ego-shattering evaluation.

My next suggestion is that on-camera teachers be given intensive training that includes not only content planning and on-camera technique but also communications theory, research findings and some exposure to McLuhan, Rand Corporation projections and even underground television. If existing teacher-

training institutions won't move fast enough—and they have shown little awareness, let alone the willingness, for initiating such programs—then I suggest we
establish the TV training for these people outside formal education. We need
to assume the responsibility for frankly and honestly admitting that at the present time, the state of the art is still pre-McGuffey reader. We must get away
from our old patterns of thinking, which are not working on television. We must
be willing to fund programs that are risk-taking and experimental. Television is
a new medium; it must be treated as such.

Dr. Mayhew of Stanford has said that the time may be near when students
without media experience will be considered illiterate. I agree with him and urge
that education at all levels offer TV-related training courses for most students
in order to eradicate "TV illiteracy" at all levels, right straight through to the
TV viewer who may say, "I don't want to take a television course." We've got
to attack on all fronts if we hope to win acceptance and do the job that must be
done to help a society that is changing at an absolutely dizzying rate.

We also need to train educational administrators in the reality of television
utilization. They must understand that this is new, that it is different, that it is
not just a camera pointed at a lesson. They must loosen their grasp on decisions
that they are incapable of making. They must learn to think visually. If the content does not lend itself to a visual presentation, then they should say, "This is
radio." And they don't do that very often! They must realize that it takes time,
energy and creativity to produce television shows. (My administrators have
naively suggested that they will offer me three units of released time for a three-
unit course I'm developing. I spend one hour for every minute I'm on television.
My television work takes me 30 or 40 hours per week in addition to my regular
work.) Finally, administrators must seek funding for television, and they must
label the funds "specifically for television," or "for cable"; for if the funds are
allocated generally, they will be dissipated through proposal-reading committees
who are not television-convinced.

My last recommendation is that you resist what I call the "myopia of mega-
lomania," which is the compulsion to think that only large-scale, Cecil B.
DeMille-type productions are worth funding. Don't forget, we are the products
of commercial television. Let's at this stage be realistic. If it took 8 million
dollars to produce "Sesame Street" to teach kids to count to 10, we'll never
get to trigonometry. This approach will scarcely nibble at the edge of a vast and
crying need for continuing education. As I've indicated, my research has shown
that viewers are very accepting of less than Academy Award-winning instructional television if the content meets their needs. I'm sustained by a quote from
Caleb Gattegno's book *Toward a Visual Culture,* in which he says the "the future
of television in education is coincident with the education of telecasters in the
use of themselves as people who can teach the dynamics of seeing, imagining
and imaging and can find in the medium the infinity of uses, known and still un-
known, of man by himself."

So I propose that no matter what effort you give to theorizing and research-
ing, to developing and executing large plans, to working out delivery systems, to

securing funding, to analyzing social needs, to perfecting cooperation between cable systems so that they can serve human needs—much of your effort will be lost if you neglect the practitioner; for we are, in the last analysis, dependent on him to produce the product which is your vehicle for continuing education.

Discussion

Gerald S. Lesser

Dr. Lesser is Charles Bigelow Professor of Education and Developmental Psychology at the Harvard Graduate School of Education. He is also chairman of the Board of Advisors of the Children's Television Workshop. In his presentation to the Aspen Workshop conference, he described the interplay between research and creative production which resulted in the development of "Sesame Street."

Sam Gould has characterized "Sesame Street" as starting with some clear educational purposes and then using highly professional technical skills to realize those purposes. Although things in actuality are never quite so linear, that succession of events basically did characterize the project. There are several ways in which our series at the Children's Television Workshop does not connect, and cannot connect, with the topic of cable and continuing education. "Sesame Street" and the other CTW programs are meant for national distribution, not community or regional distribution. Our target audience is three-, four- and five-year-olds, but I think basically we reach even younger children than that and not the older people that we're talking about here.

But I think there are also some clear connections. One is that we've gone on in the last two years to producing "The Electric Company" for slightly older audiences, trying to teach basic reading skills to elementary school kids. And we're currently planning a health series for adolescents and young adults. Even on "Sesame Street" we've been concerned right along with trying to connect, as best we could, with the parents of these young kids. Obviously no television program operates in isolation, and we've been trying hard to work with parents, especially those of the inner city, to try to reinforce what we do.

The other connection is the one that I think we're here to discuss. The Children's Television Workshop has succeeded in establishing some sort of successful partnership between television producers, on the one hand, and educators and researchers on the other. I would like to talk about the nature of that collaboration and how it's developed in our experience.

There are three types of educators. One set of educators can be thought of as users—the classroom teachers using "Electric Company," the faculties in college classrooms and so forth. Another group of educators can be thought of as suppliers—those who try to work in collaboration with the producers in order to improve the quality of the television production material. Clearly the best known function of educators, at least as they operate as researchers, is that of policemen. They come along with assessment techniques and evaluation designs and tell the people after the whole thing's over how well, or more often, how poorly they've done.

I'll be talking here about the way in which the educators have tried to act as suppliers of information about children that can be used in collaboration with the production group. This collaboration started four or five years ago with considerable skepticism, both on the part of the producers and the educators. Dave Connell, vice president in charge of production for the Children's Workshop, was the most skeptical of all. Dave says:

> *My background was in commercial television, where we felt we had developed a pretty good set of instincts about what kind of show would appeal to children at any given age. I frankly was skeptical about the idea of researching every moment of a television show and certainly of being told how to design it. There was the risk of intellectualizing the material to death and ending up with a program most notable for its monumental boredom. It would be like trying to analyze the elements of a joke, only to find out that when we had isolated all the pieces, there was nothing learned and nothing to laugh about. But if Sesame Street was an experiment, and it definitely continues to be one, this notion of educator-broadcaster cooperation was the most bold experiment within it. I kept thinking of the biologists who crossed a crocodile with an abalone in hopes of getting an abadile; only something went wrong and they ended up with a crocabalone.*

Now, like most other things in life, the successful production-educator collaboration has been a matter of personal chemistry. But beyond this personal chemistry, on-going collaboration between production and research people follows a few general principles. Both sides had to start by sharing and admitting to some psychological obstacles that we confronted. There had to be a willingness to admit at the outset that things might go wrong, that there might be the possibility that our programs would be lousy. You like to go into a project like "Sesame Street" saying, "That will never happen to us. We're not going to need these continuous self-correcting devices, because we're going to be great from the beginning." Instead, I think you have to start out with the mind-set that things are almost certain to go wrong. This is the opposite of another mind-set, which is to think that when you don't know about your kids' reactions to what you're doing, none of that can harm you.

Another obstacle can be the producers' unwillingness to share some portion of their creative autonomy. All of you know that producers feel that their good shows come out of their belly buttons—out of their instincts—and any effort to analyze, to sit around with a group of people and think about what you're doing, shares this creative autonomy and runs the great risk of demolishing it in the process.

There were other kinds of issues in producer-researcher collaboration that had to be raised from the producer's point of view. One was the simple issue of paying for your mistakes. Early in "Sesame Street" there were a great many occasions where we simply dumped material which our child observations were telling us didn't work. That is very expensive and can be a shaky kind of experience for the producer. And on the educator/researcher side, there are many traditions that had to be either given up or modified in order to collaborate successfully with producers. Most researchers have played the role of policeman more often than the role of one who tries actively to serve production in a collaborative fashion. This is one of the roles that they had to give up. The role of *guru*, considering himself the source of all educational wisdom, is another that the educator and the researcher had to give up. They had to find ways of thinking through the educational ideas—what to teach, how to teach it, what kind of kids are we dealing with, and so forth—and then they had to figure out how to share all of those ideas with the other creative people involved.

The timing and pace of research contains other traditions that had to be modified. In doing research studies, you try to be extremely careful; you try to replicate your studies, you try to take your time. In working with production on a day-to-day basis, the researcher can't do that. You know that you're going to get sloppy, and you try to work within those constraints as best you can. You give up large samples; you give up statistical tests of significance. There aren't many researchers who are trained to give up all of those traditional research functions and immediately communicate to the producers what they have learned from kids watching the televised materials.

Four years later, all of this is still going on; and I think by now we would have found that if this collaboration wasn't working for us because it was so time-consuming and so expensive, we would have given up. But both sides regard it as absolutely essential to the Workshop's success. We still spend a lot of time working together on a day-to-day basis. The Workshop has now produced over 500 one-hour "Sesame Street" programs. We are at the end of our fourth broadcasting year and are now planning for the fifth. For this fifth year, we are in intensive curriculum discussions between the producers and the educators and are thinking of going in a very different direction. We've also produced 260 half-hour "Electric Company" programs, and we'll be beginning its third broadcast year in the fall.

Let me touch lastly on the matter of expense and financing. There are certain clear expenses involved. First, if you're going to have researchers do these kinds of things, you're going to have to hire them. Since there are no traditional training procedures to get researchers to go beyond the role of policeman, they've got to spend some time in on-the-job training, or at least in learning the job themselves. There also are enormous expenses, as I mentioned a moment ago, in modifying and sometimes abandoning material that has already been produced. You try it on groups of kids before you ever begin broadcasting or before you ever put it on the air. If you find it's beyond modification, you simply have to dump it, and obviously there is a lot of expense involved in that. From our point of view all of those expenses have been worth it in reflecting on the quality of the programs we produce.

Discussion

Norman E. Watson

Dr. Watson is chancellor of the Coast Community College District in Orange County, California. The district is made up of two colleges, Golden West and Orange Coast, both of which are heavily committed to the exploration of innovative teaching methods. Dr. Watson is also president of KOCE-TV, the district's own UHF educational television station, which began operating in November 1972. In his presentation to the conference, Dr. Watson described a number of experiments at the two colleges in the use of educational technology.

Our primary objectives in using technology in the Coast Community College District were, first, to reach more people in different ways, and, second, to do a more effective job in instruction and in education. Thus, during the past several years we have been exploring a number of new learning modes. We have gone heavily into the audio-tutorial mode at one of our institutions, where we have opened labs for students in a number of different disciplines. We have located terminals on both of our college campuses and now have about 280 operational CAI [Computer Assisted Instruction] programs. We have also a large night program—more than 50 percent of the district's 40,000 students attend during the evening.

In 1966, we were fortunate to have an educational channel allocated to Orange County. Since that time we worked persistently to have the channel allocated to the Coast Community College District. We were finally successful in persuading the people east of the Mississippi that there was some activity in Southern California other than growing oranges and surfing, and we did get the channel allocated to the district. We invested about 3 million dollars in production facilities, purchasing the best commercial quality equipment that was available and building a staff of 32 producers, technicians, artists, directors and writers from the commercial stations in our vicinity. Then, on November 20, 1972, Channel 50 went on the air as a comprehensive UHF color station serving the 1.6 million people in our county as well as an additional 6 million people from San Diego to Los Angeles.

Channel 50 greatly increases our ability to reach more people. There are many things we still do not know about educational television and so we are presently experimenting with a great many different models for non-traditional studies. One thing we do know, however, is that educational television is ready to rise above the programming level of the last two decades. Educational television has gone beyond the point it was at a few years ago. I am reminded of a *New Yorker* cartoon in which the college dean takes the visiting fireman into the lecture hall, where 2,000 students are sitting in class, nodding and passive. A television camera beams on the lecture and the dean says, "Isn't technology wonderful?" Educational television must rise to a new plateau.

I would like to describe some of the ways we are trying to reach this goal. First, cooperative relationships are fundamental in achieving the kind of quality results that are going to pay off in the area of ETV. As a member of the Southern California TV Consortium, consisting of 26 community colleges in Southern California, we have discovered that there is strength in numbers and cooperation. We have combined forces to produce two television courses per year. Our first year's enrollment, when we had only 12 members, was about 1,200 students; and the first courses we selected were the over-subscribed, over-enrolled, fairly traditional programs in the institutions. Although the mode of delivery was non-traditional, the selection of the content of the courses was not. However, we are attempting additional models as time goes on.

Another program that has a great deal more risk and a great many more problems is Project Outreach. It is an attempt to bring together the three segments of higher education in California—the community colleges, the state college and university system, and the University of California—to cooperate in producing educational programs on a regional basis. Since these three segments have never really joined on anything else before, this has not been an easy project. There have been all kinds of difficulties with respect to credentials, credits, fees, course approvals, faculty senate involvement. We are fortunate in having some individuals working with us who are most receptive and innovative. What we hope to do is develop programs and program segments that will be of sufficiently high quality that they may be used by all the various segments.

Project Access is another program we are involved in with the College of San Mateo district, the Chicago TV College, and Miami-Dade Community College. What we are attempting to do here is have each district produce a quality course with the assistance and counsel of both the content people and the technicians at cooperating institutions. Each institution that produces one course will in turn receive courses from the others.

At the same time, we are also producing courses independently. The first course we produced was an introductory psychology course called "As Man Behaves." We had an instructor who was well-equippped to handle the course, and we brought in such people as Carl Rogers and B.F. Skinner as participants in the program. The second course we've attempted is cultural anthropology, which we are shooting in 30 countries throughout the world. Here, we were fortunate to have the backing of the National Endowment for the Humanities.

Another model that we are exploring—which probably has as much if not more potential than any of the others—is a series of modularized learning packages. We are attempting to develop these with intrinsic values, so that each module can stand alone. Each module will include televison, radio, correspondence material, texts, syllabi, workbooks, computer programs and evaluation instruments, all designed as coherent wholes. They will be augmented by campus facilitators, field experiences and on-campus seminars. In the course-development process, we are bringing together broad participation from institutions nationwide, so that at the very outset we will have input from a wide number of individuals who will later be users of the product. They will represent the content specialists from various disciplines—producers, directors, writers, and technical specialists. We hope to use the team approach in the preparation of these materials and to build continuous assessment and evaluation into the program. The last component in this will consist of workshops on the use of the products.

As I have said, we don't know which of these models will work best. We are trying a lot of different approaches and will learn as we go along.

Discussion

Jack McBride

Mr. McBride is manager of the Nebraska ETV Network, headquartered in the Nebraska Educational Telecommunications Center in Lincoln. The center also houses the Nebraska Educational Television Council for Higher Education (NETCHE) and the Great Plains National ITV Library and is a focal point for research in and utilization of educational television. In 1972, Mr. McBride was appointed special assistant to the president of the University of Nebraska and executive director of the State University of Nebraska (S-U-N) project, which he described in the following presentation to the Aspen Workshop conference.

S-U-N has great potential applicability to many of the areas this conference is discussing. The State University of Nebraska is a research project at this point in time, but we are currently developing the tools needed to move into a demonstration phase, with substantial funding over a number of years.

We've been in instructional television in this country since the early 1950s. You can chart the development of American instructional television from the early days, which broadcast little more than the talking face; through the next phase, which was the illustrated lecture; through the phase that involved taking the program out of the studio by means of film and remote crews; to the current phase, which is developing the substantial consortial funding required to achieve quality professional production. Anticipating this rapidly developing trend toward continuing education, open learning and non-traditional instruction, the University of Nebraska prepared a proposal which led to an Office of Education planning grant two years ago. We currently have a substantial research and development grant from the National Center for Educational Technology to determine two things: first, how to employ the several educational technologies systematically in a new, non-traditional delivery system; and second, how to design and produce college level materials of significant quality, usable in a number of areas across the country by a variety of educational institutions.

After having examined all of the non-traditional systems and projects and plans across the country and throughout the world, we have designed, produced and tested a number of specific pilot materials. We are attempting to bring the first and second years of credit college courses to students of all ages who will not or are not able to attend college on a traditional campus. Our target audience is well-defined, since we have engaged in considerable research and market studies concerning our potential clientele. Who is the audience available? It's the adult. Who is the adult? A wide gamut of people, from the high school senior who has taken all the courses in his small school's curriculum and is bored with his final year of high school or wants to get a head start into college, all the way up the continuum to the senior citizen.

We find, through our own surveys—now being substantiated by professional research and measurement firms—that there is a definite clientele interested in paying to take these college courses. Indeed, after proceeding through a systematic and somewhat sophisticated process to eliminate those who agree that education, like the Deity and Motherhood, is good, we find that if such media-oriented courses were available tomorrow, 2 percent of the population would take $15 out of their pockets for each credit hour and actually enroll in these courses. This is being corroborated by the professional firms working now with a much larger sample than the interview and questionnaire samples we developed locally. Our last year's study was within the State of Nebraska; our current study is the Midwest. Thus, we are talking about rather substantial sums if these projections are sustained.

S-U-N, among other things, means a new development process for courseware. Each S-U-N course is composed of lessons which themselves have six parts: (1) a television program module—be it broadcast, cable or video cassette, (2) an audio cassette module, (3) a syllabus module, (4) a textual module, (5) an instructional kit module, and (6) a newspaper lesson module—we have been working with several newspapers in the Midwest which are committed to including an introductory article dealing with the lesson on the day that lesson is to be broadcast. These six modules interrelate systematically by design to provide total instruction. In addition, a certain measure of redundancy is built in, so that even if the non-traditional student, undisciplined by the classroom setting, does not avail himself of all six modules, he will still achieve his goal. He will still do at least as well as his counterpart in the classroom.

The S-U-N project has developed an elaborate new five-phase process for the design of courses. The process consists of research leading into an initial design phase; followed by a production phase; followed by a rigorous field-testing phase— we have borrowed liberally from the Children's Television Workshop and its formative and summative research and production process; followed by re-design; and then followed by re-production based upon the findings from this elaborate field testing. Through this process, it will take 12 to 18 months to develop a single course. But we believe that everything this conference wishes to achieve will fail miserably unless we develop a quality instructional televison product.

There are several other significant aspects to this plan as well. Beyond providing successful quality programming in both "Sesame Street" and "The Electric Company," CTW has left three legacies to all those working with instructional technology: (1) CTW showed that it takes substantial dollars to produce the kind of professional quality programs usable throughout the country. (2) CTW developed a way to marry research and production by means of (a) formative research, which is testing the production phase to assist in changing the design of the product before using it, and (b) summative research, which is seriously testing the product upon completion and then, based upon the findings, improving it even more. (3) CTW showed that the instruction must be designed specifically to the medium being employed.

The chief reasons why American instructional television has advanced no further than it has, particularly at the higher education level, are faculty apathy and antagonism, the lack of significant dollars committed to production, and the fact that the assets and advantages inherent in the television medium were not being employed. What we were doing was using television simply to mirror traditional education. The colege professor, the instructor or the classroom teacher came into the studio to do exactly what he had done in the classroom. If we were lucky, the television producer would convince the professor to use a couple of visuals. "Sesame Street" was the first proven example where this was significantly changed. The faculty members, the content authorities, the content specialists did not have veto power over program design but rather went into the project knowing that, while content would be essential and there would be great reliance upon content advisors, final decisions would be made by the television producers. This marked the first time in American instructional television that content was designed expressly to the medium.

We have attempted with the S-U-N project to employ all these legacies. We are developing course and production teams of professionals that strive from the outset both to identify the particular role and responsibility of each one of the lesson modules and to design the modules specifically to the particular medium.

A typical course team is composed of senior content specialist consultants from across the country, a professional producer, an educational psychologist, an instructional design specialist, an audio producer, two writers, a cinematographer, and appropriate art, graphics, film, television and technical support services. All are systematically employed to address themselves to teaching and learning in this non-traditional setting.

We're highly encouraged by the results thus far. We wouldn't begin to say that we know all that there is to know. As a result of research, we know a great deal about how not to employ technology in adult education, and slowly we're learning how to proceed systematically. But there are some very interesting and exciting things happening with this project. If we can bring together a triumverate of content specialists, educational researchers and top television and other media professionals, and if we can define which specialties are needed, what the responsibilities of each member of the team should be and how they should relate one to the other in order to do an academically effective job, we could have a formula which conceivably could produce validated instructional materials in any subject matter at any level, credit or non-credit, continuing education or other.

Our delivery system is designed to broadcast the television modules over the Nebraska state network system in prime time, with a repeat of each lesson on the weekend. As we look to the future, we can quickly run out of broadcast time; so, obviously, this system will have to turn rapidly to cable systems as a prime means of distribution of the television module of these courses. One of the things we want to start testing early next year is providing all course instruction to the student in his home. We are going to contrast that with student use of nearby resource or learning centers, where all of the modules, including video and audio cassettes, will be available to the student. In this kind of setting, the student is no longer lock-stepped to a broadcast or a distribution schedule or to the traditional academic semester. In this kind of a setting, a student can start the course any time he wants during the year, can proceed at his own pace, can take the examination, and then if he passes, can receive the credit.

We are anticipating no prerequisites. We couldn't care less what the academic background of the student is. If he enrolls, pays his tuition and successfully completes the course, he is awarded credit. We are planning a toll-free telephone line 24 hours a day to allow the student to call in at any time he is troubled, is working on his assignments or has questions or needs counseling. A counselor would be located at each of the resource centers in the event the student wanted to take that approach instead.

Obviously this is going to cost money, as anything of quality will. Indeed, the only way to make this work is to see that the materials produced are so academically sound and so professionally prepared that they can be leased by colleges and universities anywhere across the country. We have found, in our research, great receptivity to the concept. Our plan is to package these course modules and then let other universities use them in whatever configuration they want. We will encourage educational institutions and agencies in other states to distribute the courses and modules in whatever distribution fashion they deem appropriate.

We are to the point of serious discussions with the Mid-America State Universities Association, a compact of state universities in this midwestern region. It is highly conceivable that S-U-N could actually become what the Newman Report and the Carnegie Commission referred to as a "regional university." S-U-N has the potential, we believe, within five years to evolve into a University of Mid-America.

Discussion

Jessie Hartline

Dr. Hartline is acting dean of University College at Rutgers University and is also director of Rutgers' Open University Project, one of four such projects in the United States which are experimenting with the use of course materials from the British Open University. In her remarks to the Aspen Workshop conference, Dean Hartline described how she became involved with the use of educational media, the initial results from the Open University Project, and her plans for expanded use of educational media at Rutgers.

Three years ago, the main purpose in my getting involved in any kind of media or non-traditional study was simply to improve the quality of the courses that I was teaching. At that time, I was teaching economics and was aware of its reputation as the "dismal science." It seemed that there were a great many resources with which to teach better and more interestingly in addition to the books, blackboard, chalk and even the slides that I was using. I thought that I could use the reality of economic phenomena existing in daily life in the State of New Jersey and also invite important economists, such as the Council of Economic Advisors of the state, to be a part of my courses. These ideas, of course, could only be implemented through the use of media.

I made a proposal for a one-year program on economic issues to the public broadcasting authorities. The response at that time was that because of inadequate funds for programming, my project could not be funded and that only programs of general appeal to the public could be financed. Though I pointed out that even though my economics series may have low viewing by the general public, the potential use of the series by community and state colleges, as well as my own use in the university, made it a much more attractive proposal. Still, the funding and interest were not there.

As a result of my discussion and meetings, however, I was asked to host and be economics commentator on an hour-long TV documentary every week for a year. It was quite an experience. It made very clear to me the expenses and complications of television production. One cannot just say to public broadcasting or cable people, "I'm going to put this course together," and think that that is the end of it and it will just happen. I think a lot of us in academics several years ago thought things were that simple. Televised education is an immensely time-consuming and difficult process.

Sometime later, I decided that if the use of public television was out, I would join others who were working and involved with television on the closed-circuit, on-campus ITV center. The "others" were a very few young faculty members; this tremendous investment in hardware was getting only marginal use. Again, the work we found was enormous and it had to be done on an extra workload basis. I began asking the various departments if they would like to join us in using audio-visual media, and, generally, the responses were favorable. Then I asked who was interested in creating programs, and I got a few nibbles. Once they got a look at what was involved, however, I got mainly negative responses. The answer seemed to be that the instructors wanted existing courseware, and very soon I was in the module business.

Armed with a very thick catalogue of available courseware nationally, I again went to interested faculty. The faculty would have had bifocals on by the time they finished carefully looking through this catalogue, and they would have been blind if they had tried to review all the potentially interesting films. The module scene at this point in time is incredible—a vast array of material available with not one clue as to whether it is any good or not. The departments have to review them and agree that module X is better than module Y, and this process is extraordinarily difficult. I think modules created and used on a consortia basis might be able to succeed, but for the faculty of a major university to go out and try to make a large-scale breakthrough using existing modules just may not be possible.

The feeling then prevailed that it would be easier and more preferable to create multi-media courses *de novo* than go through the review, cut and paste process. The intent, by this time, was not only to improve the quality of instruction but also to reach new constituencies who could not or would not attend classes on campus. Thinking the problem through, I also felt there should be an additional requirement for the non-traditional programs. There must be a high degree of academic credibility and, thus, transferability. Rutgers University College, the part-time degree-granting College of Rutgers, has a 60 percent transfer student body. We are the most densely populated state in the nation; we are the most industrialized. We have people coming in and going out all the time. We know very well the importance of transferability, credibility and common currency of college credits. We cannot, in good faith, offer anything in the curriculum that is not going to have the assurance of full faith for the credits when the student moves on. If we are going to reach that "new" student, we must be honest and fair with him and offer a good quality program.

The enormous expense of resources for us to create the quality programming we wanted seemed to me a major, and possibly unnecessary, difficulty. But, to gain faculty and student support, proven quality courses already put together had to be sought out. The solution that I came upon is what I now call the "Leader Institution" concept. We began looking at the Open University materials and saw that the "Leader Institutions" of Oxford, Edinburgh and Cambridge, among others, were reviewing and examining the students in the British Open University. No faculty could say that this was inferior, and they wouldn't tell me that obviously we can do it significantly better, because this material has been internationally reviewed. There are ways that it might be modified, but the bulk of the material is there, and the bulk is good. We began by asking faculty committees to review these materials, and they have done so. Three programs have been passed. The faculty is giving 15 credit hours for each course. (I am assuming that you know the format of the Open University.)

There were two additional things that I thought were important considerations for the program. One is that the program would not be a totally television-oriented thing. The television is used where it ought to be used. It's not merely the talking head, not merely the substitute for the classroom. Instead, it is doing appropriate things with television, such as showing the inside of an atom or a scene from the Old Vic—bringing something to the student that he could not get in the classroom. Even in the math program, a computer mapping function is shown to illustrate how this relates to airplane wing design. I believe that this course embodies the use of the television as it should be used.

As for radio, they have used radio in such a way as to humanize the possibilities for the student, When I was in London, I listened to one of their programs on which they had scheduled a lecture by a foremost scientist. Instead, I heard "We have postponed Dr. So-and-So's lecture because your homework assignments last week were terribly disappointing. Would you please get out your papers." They had a panel of three of the science faculty review and explain the problems. It wasn't just a canned lecture. Although it is one-way, there was a two-way feeling about what they were doing with the medium.

The work of the overall program is very difficult and demanding. It is not intended for the educationally disadvantaged in any way. This is a special program for a different but important student—the adult student who could use an appropriate chance to go to school. There are lots of adults who have the same capability as the adults who can get to the classroom. They are the housewives who went to school many years ago and now want to go back, the Vietnam veterans, the elderly, the institutionalized. They are all the non-traditional students that we have been talking about.

So, with the adoption of the program, we set up various policies. There are no entrance requirements whatsoever. Students need show us no credentials, no background, nothing at all. The only requirement was one I insisted on: that every student must talk with a professor before enrolling. This meant not a guidance counselor, not a registrar, but a professor who could explain the nature of the course and show them the material. As a matter of fact, that is how we got the data for the correlation of motivation to other characteristics of the students who are now in the program. The professor who interviewed the student would put a little note at the bottom of the card—"motivated," in their opinion, or "not motivated." The student didn't see this. We found that the single most important characteristic for success is high motivation, and it has nothing to do with age, schooling, background, sex or geographic location.

The students range in age from 16 to 65, from high school students to retired people. Over 60 percent are women; 17 percent are black. Another study took a random sample of those who called and inquired but did not sign up. Of that group, only 2 percent of the blacks who inquired did not sign up. The other thing that we found was that people over 45 had a large no-show syndrome. However when we asked these no-shows "Would you be interested next year?", only 4 percent said, "Absolutely not." So we feel that older people may simply watch and see and take their time.

We are now offering the math, sciences and humanities courses. We hope to extend that in the future. Our evaluation is now half-way through. I can tell you one interesting thing we found in comparing the American with the English student: In the math course, the complaints and difficulties arose in the exact same units that the British students found difficult and/or dull. In a negative way, this seemed to say that there is not that much difference between the students on both sides.

We are only showing the television programs on film at the study center. We really couldn't use public televison. Last year, WNET in New York offered us prime-time for the program, but it was impossible to take it. We didn't have the resources to risk exposure to a potential audience of 7½ million over New York television, and we had no cable possibilities that I knew of at that time. Every supplementary sheet, every test, every single item had to be imported from England because there was no American distributor. We are, therefore, relying on the study centers, where the programs are shown via film weekly. Associate professors in the discipline are at the study centers when the unit calls for that discipline. The films are readily available and the students can come in anytime.

There is another aspect of this that I think we ought to recognize. In the science course, the films are vital in order to do the experiments. In the math course, we think the films are extraordinarily helpful, although we have one math student in Alaska and another in South Dakota who are obviously not seeing the films. The humanities film series is primarily enrichment. We hope the students view them and we want them to, but it is possible not to see the humanities films and still get by. We find that two-thirds of the students are coming to the centers with some regularity, and they are beginning to pace themselves in their work. Our drop-out rate so far is very low—approximately 22 percent. We think that is quite good.

Where do we go from here? Well, first of all there are going to have to be some adaptations. We are going to have to rewrite the social science course. We have our own plan. The faculty for this kind of work must be dedicated teachers. To rely solely on academic stars would be a mistake, in my view. Who are our stars in higher education? They are not stars because they are brilliant teachers; they are generally stars in spite of the fact that they are teachers. They get to be stars because they publish and they construct theoretical constructs that add to the body of knowledge, and this is vitally important. Use the academic stars to appraise, lecture or comment, but rely on teachers who are vitally dedicated to put the courses together. My rule for the program to date has been that no one should work in this program unless they want to. You cannot have reluctant people doing something that requires this much work. I believe you have got to have people chosen for their teaching, dedication and enthusiasm.

Now, what can cable do? First of all, cable can give me a specific audience—a controlled audience that I can reach and with which I can have a two-way communication. I'm not going to worry about the technology. We've got to use cable where it can be used best, and that is for an audience that I can communicate with even by postcard. An additional advantage in cable is that cable can provide time to show the programs several times each week. That is very important.

New Jersey is somewhat unusual in that we do not have one major newspaper covering the state. We also don't have one major New Jersey radio station. Further, we don't have one major New Jersey television channel. Cable can solve another of these problems. At present, because of the availability of excess channel time, cable can also give me radio time—audio without the visual. This may not be realistic in the long run, but it solves the radio broadcasting problem now. My cable experience has been positive so far. I met with the manager of the Morristown cable system, and he was very cooperative. We may eventually be broadcasting Open University programs on that system.

There is confidence that the educational materials are good. I'm not feeling experimental about the materials. There is good student-faculty contact, good media use, and a high degree of flexibility. We hope to use cable eventually as an additional experiment with a delivery system that they are not using in the United Kingdom. So, from my point of view, there have been all kinds of stumbling blocks, but the outcome has been good. I feel we have a very good opportunity to develop an entire degree program relatively quickly. It will have a high degree of credibility and transferability. We will be reaching new students with the multi-media approach to higher education. And I think cable is going to be part of it.

The Cable as an Educational Delivery System

3

The rapid growth of cable in this country is beginning to create an alternative distribution system which offers exciting new possibilities for the uses of television in education. The idea of cable as a medium in its own right is a recent one, however. The first CATV systems were, as the initials "CATV" imply, community television antennas. They sprang up only a few years after the inception of broadcast television to enhance television signals in areas where reception was poor or nonexistent. Over the past two decades, CATV systems have spread steadily in such areas, as well as in areas where additional imported channels carried by cable have attracted subscribers. From the first few systems in 1948, cable had reached 1 million homes via 1,000 systems by 1963; and by 1972, 2,800 systems were serving over 6 million homes, or nearly 10 percent of all television households in the United States. Currently, over 80,000 new subscribers are being added to cable systems every month. Predictions of the number of cable subscribers by the end of the decade range from a low of 15 million to a high of 40 million.

In the recent past, public interest in cable has been growing even more rapidly than the cable systems themselves. A steady stream of reports, proposals and conferences have created an awareness that a cable system is capable of providing not only more channels of conventional television but also new kinds of programming and telecommunications services. The long list of potential uses has attracted the interest of groups as diverse as municipal officials, educators, librarians, community organizers and city planners—all of whom believe that cable can help them deal more effectively with their particular concerns.

Despite all of this interest and promise, cable remains today essentially a broadcast reception service. The nature of the thinking about cable has changed more than the actual uses of cable. It seems clear, however, that if cable is to continue to grow, cable programming will have to be diversified. And if cable is to succeed in the largest urban markets, where 80 percent of the population lives and where broadcast television reception is generally good, systems will have to provide new services to attract urban subscribers.

An important guide to cable's near-term future was provided in the Federal Communication Commission's cable television rules, which went into effect on March 31, 1972. These rules deal with the number and nature of broadcast signals a cable system may carry, with minimum technical standards, and with franchising provisions. They also require that all new systems in the 100 largest television markets have

- at least a 20-channel capacity;
- one channel reserved for non-broadcast use for each broadcast signal carried;
- three free channels—one for educational use, one for municipal government and one for public access;
- additional channels available for lease;
- a built-in two-way capacity, although actual two-way service is not now required.

The implications of these rules for the use of cable in continuing education include the following:

1. Cable operators know that they need to develop new non-broadcast services in order to grow in the major markets. However, their principal focus today is on building new systems, and nearly all of the capital available to the industry in the next few years will be used for system construction. Consequently, educators should expect to take the initiative in producing and implementing an educational program on cable. Operators are generally eager for independently produced quality programming which will fill up empty channels and attract new audiences.

2. With the construction of new systems in the major markets, the number of non-broadcast channels available for use will increase rapidly; and the 1972 FCC rules assure that at least half of all channels will be reserved for non-broadcast use, the majority of these for lease. It is widely assumed that this "television of abundance" should permit programming to cater to specialized audiences and meet specialized needs, but the experience of UHF television has revealed that the simple existence of channel capacity does not mean that it will automatically be used. The specific mechanisms for the use of these cable channels for education—or for other new services— remain to be devised.

3. The FCC has mandated an educational access channel in all major market systems, leaving final authority over use of the channel in the hands of the cable operator. How well this will work in practice remains to be seen. For

example, cable operators seem to have given little thought to the possibility of their having to decide between competing claims by different educational institutions for the same time period on the educational-access channel. Nonetheless, an entire channel reserved expressly for educational purposes should provide new opportunities for experimentation. It should, for example, permit the repetition of course programming at different times during the day to reach a wider audience. If educational uses of cable grow beyond the capacity of a single channel, the FCC rules also assure the availability of additional channels for lease to educational programming.

4. The FCC requirement for two-way capacity in new systems is an attempt to encourage development of wholly new interactive services. Widespread applications of two-way cable are still perhaps a decade away due primarily to the high cost of terminal equipment and software. However, when interactive cable is available, it will certainly enhance the prospects for the delivery of a wide range of educational services to the home. Some planners feel that computer-based, individualized instruction disseminated by two-way cable will eventually provide significant portions of the educational process, both inside and outside the schools. Any successful educationl program must provide opportunity for student inquiries and feedback, of course, and until two-way cable is available, other forms of two-way communication—telephone, mail, face-to-face contact—are vital in educational television courses.

Until very recently, educators have paid little attention to cable; for with but a few (municipally owned) exceptions, cable systems have been built and operated as reception services for broadcast television and as commercial, profit-making enterprises. Just how recent is the idea of using cable for education is strikingly illustrated by the case of Vincennes University. This two-year Indiana college has been described by its president, Dr. Isaac Beckes, as "a pioneer in cable TV." The school has in fact built and operated cable systems in Vincennes and three neighboring communities since 1964. However, these are conventional CATV systems which the college runs simply to generate revenues to support an educational UHF station donated to the college in 1961. While the cable-supported ETV station now provides a range of programming from PBS, the Indiana Higher Education Television Service, and the local community, the cable system simply offers "10 different (broadcast) television channels and a weather and temperature channel." Only now, after eight years of operation, are plans underway to offer "special local programming" on the cable.*

The evidence available suggests that the evolution of CATV toward a true communications system serving a variety of special purposes will be neither quick nor simple, and it will require extraordinary cooperation among cable operators and their potential customers. The problems of bringing continuing education to

---

*Isaac Beckes, "Vincennes University: Pioneer in Cable TV." *Community and Junior College Journal,* Vol. 43, No. 3, November 1972, pp. 10-11.

the cable are largely problems of adopting a system developed for one purpose—broadcast reception—to another, more specialized use. These same problems will be involved in the implementation of many other new cable services, whether it be public access, utilizing a municipal government channel, or the use of cable by the public schools, libraries or physicians. The most immediate problems relating to the use of cable for continuing education are

1. the complexities of gaining access to cable systems;
2. the limited extent of cable penetration;
3. the inadequate demographics for cable systems;
4. the lowly status of cablecasting;
5. the lack of interconnection of cable systems.

1. *Gaining access to cable.* The 1972 FCC cable rules require an "educational access channel" as part of all new cable systems within the top 100 markets. According to the rules, the channel is to be available for use without charge for a period of five years from the inauguration of service. The commission explains that this free channel has been designated "to encourage innovation in educational uses of television" and that it expects the channel to be used for "institutional programming and other educational purposes." The rules themselves state only that the channel shall be available "for use by local educational authorities"; that advertising, lottery information, and obscene or indecent matter are prohibited; and that the cable system must keep a complete record of "all persons or groups requesting access time" for public inspection. No mechanisms are established for administering the channel, for deciding among competing claims for time on the channel, or for determining who qualifies as "local educational authorities." The ultimate judgments on these matters presumably rest with the cable operators, since the rules state explicitly that "except on specific [FCC] authorization . . . no local entity shall prescribe any other rules concerning the number or the manner of operation of access channels."

Although active competiton for use of the educational channel is unlikely in the initial phase of implementation, it seems logical that something like the "nondiscriminatory, first-come, first-served" requirement on the public-access channel would also be applied to the educational-access channel. A second alternative would be for the operator to request FCC approval to set up an Educational Access Commission made up of representatives of agencies interested in using the channel. Such a solution should be attractive to operators, since it would alleviate them of the administrative responsibility for a channel from which they can derive no revenue.

Cable systems in markets below the top 100 are not required to provide the three free-access channels, although the communities served by the systems are given the option of requiring such channels in their franchises. No community, however, may require *more* than a single free educational or public access or municipal channel without special approval from the FCC. And to obtain this approval, the local community would have to make a "special showing" to the commission which clearly indicates both the need for additional free channels and the ability to use them. The commission is apparently concerned that local communities will make unreasonable demands which may threaten the economic viability of new cable systems. Consequently, the commission seems likely to approve such plans only in circumstances where a strong case is made (by both the operator and the community) for exceeding the FCC requirements.

Since a cable franchise may be granted for a period of up to 15 years, it is important that educators (and other community groups) recognize their stake in the development of cable and exert some influence in the planning and development of their local system. Although the FCC has sharply limited local jurisdiction over the access channels, the manifest willingness of a franchise applicant to work cooperatively with the educational community should be made a factor in choosing the franchisee. And prudence suggests that competing cable operators' statements of good intentions be checked against actual performance in other communities in which the operators already have systems.

During the pre-franchise phase, it is vital that educators not only think about what they want from a cable system but also consider realistically how they will use such a system. The FCC rules require only that a channel be available for educational purposes; it is the responsibility of those who wish to use the channel to provide the production facilities and personnel. If courses or other kinds of educational programming are prepared on tape or film, provision must be made for playback facilities at the cable system. If a course is to be presented live, then arrangements must be made either to use a cable system studio or to link the point of origination (*e.g.,* an on-campus TV studio) with the cable head end, either via cable or microwave. If the head end is remote from the desired originating point, the cost for the educational producers can be high.

So far we have been considering only the issue of ensuring access to new cable systems. Gaining access to older systems raises a different set of problems. Systems already in operation or licensed by the FCC prior to March 31, 1972, are "grandfathered" for a five-year period—that is, they are not required to be in compliance with the new rules for five years so long as they continue to offer the same services they did prior to the issuance of the rules. Thus, these systems are required to provide free access channels only if they wish to add *new* broadcast signals to their service.

These facts certainly do not preclude the possibility of access to older cable systems. An earlier FCC ruling required all cable systems with more than 3,500 subscribers to offer "a significant amount" of locally originated programming. This ruling, which was upheld by the Supreme Court in 1972, means that at least one channel in the larger systems will already be available for cablecasting. Since most operators have limited funds and personnel available for programming, they may well welcome outside programming from the educational community to help them meet this requirement. These operators may also be willing to work with educators and even to provide studio space or technical assistance. Systems with fewer than 3,500 subscribers may also produce programming, but it is usually on an extremely modest scale. At present, the majority of cable systems, old and new, still act simply as community antenna reception services, with perhaps one automated time and weather information channel.

Another problem with older cable systems is their limited channel capacity. A 1972 survey of cable systems in California revealed that of the 245 systems contacted, 193 had a capacity of 12 or fewer channels. And according to *TV Factbook*, the channel capacity of all the nation's systems, as of March 1972, was as follows:

over 12	361
6-12	2,026
5 only	323
under 5	55

Increasing the capacity of the smaller systems can be a costly undertaking which may require laying a second cable or replacing large numbers of amplifiers. But there are other simple and inexpensive ways to use such a system for educational programming. The cable system in Amarillo, Texas, for example, offers only six channels of broadcast programming, with no local origination other than an automated weather channel and news ticker. However, the cable system has strung a cable from its head end to the television studio of Amarillo (Community) College, and the college cablecasts two for-credit courses over the system by inserting its programming for an hour each evening on the weather channel. Since the insertion of course programming onto the channel is handled entirely by the college, the only expense to the operator has been the initial cost of providing the cable link.*

2. *Extent of cable penetration.* Just about 10 percent of all American Homes, or 6.5 million, are now receiving television by means of cable. While this is a substantial number of subscribers, they are divided among 2,800 cable systems across the country, so that the average cable system has approximately 2,100 subscribers. Actual systems range in size from several hundred with under 500 subscribers to a handful with more than 40,000†—numbers which are quite small in comparison to the reach of broadcast television stations.

Moreover, cable penetration—the ratio of actual subscribers to homes within

---

*The Amarillo College program demonstrates another important principle for educators striving for television distribution. A cable system can also be thought of as a *supplement* to broadcast television, not just as an alternative. That is, course programming can be broadcast and taped at the times available on local stations (for commercial stations, this usually means the early morning hours). Then the tape can be repeated once or more at more convenient times via a cable channel. The courses from Amarillo College are distributed in precisely this way.

†According to *TV Factbook* figures of July 1972, the largest system in the country, in San Diego, had 65,000 subscribers.

reach of cable systems—approaches 100 percent only in those communities in which over-the-air reception is extremely poor or nonexistent. Penetration in cities where more stations are available and reception is generally good tends to be much lower. For the San Diego system, it is approximately 50 percent (based in part on signals imported from Los Angeles); for the TelePrompTer system in New York, approximately 30 percent; for San Francisco, just under 30 percent. The average penetration for all systems nationally is slightly more than 50 percent. The problems of cable penetration in the cities is clearly demonstrated by a 1971 survey of interest in cable in Washington, D.C. A team from Howard University found that

> *Even at a subscriber fee of $3.50 a month—significantly lower than the $5 to $6 a month being charged by most cable systems now in operation—only 18 percent to 33 percent of Washington residents could be expected to subscribe to a cable system offering a conventional assortment of services, such as are offered by many cable systems, but without the importation of distant signals. Subscribership would rise only slightly if two distant signals were added. Such levels of subscribership would not be adequate either to make the system economically viable or to enable it to perform any significant amount of local and community service.* *

What additional services will be required to attract non-subscribers to cable is one of the most important unanswered questions facing the cable industry today. Clearly, the problem will not be solved by offering courses for continuing education on cable, or by any other single form of programming. If cable is to flourish in the cities, it will have to appeal to a variety of interests. And the desire for further education is certainly one of these interests.

In any case, for the immediate future, educators interested in cable must deal with the fact that only a fraction of the population can now be reached by cable programming. One simple immediate means for dealing with cable's limited penetration is to set up cable viewing sites at accessible locations within a community. Schools, churches, cultural and recreational centers are logical sites for group viewing. In suburban areas, shopping centers are increasingly becoming centers for social interaction and entertainment as well as commerce, and these centers should offer interesting possibilities for both live and televised education. Other possible solutions to the problem of limited penetration are treated below in the following sections dealing with cable demographics, the status of cablecasting, and the need for interconnection of systems.

3. *Demographics of cable.* We have been emphasizing throughout this discussion that cable grew essentially as a reception service, which means that the most

---

*Ralph Lee Smith, "Ownership Policy and the Cable Industry." *Yale Review of Law and Social Action,* Spring 1972, pp. 266-267.

widely shared characteristic of cable subscribers up to the present is an interest in better television reception and a wider choice of channels. There is evidence, however, that at least some cable subscribers are interested in more than old movies and clearer reception of the latest situation comedy. The Hughes Aircraft Corporation recently surveyed the interests of cable subscribers in various kinds of programming not now available on television. The corporation was interested in programming that could be disseminated nationally by a Hughes-built and -operated communications satellite. The survey revealed that a small but significant percentage of cable subscribers were interested enough in opera, in legitimate theater, in ballet and in instruction in such skills as ceramics, painting and guitar-playing that they were willing to pay several dollars a month to receive it via pay-cable. According to the survey, 8 percent of the audience would pay up to $4 per month for a series of operas, 5 percent would pay for a London Theater series, and 5 percent for a ballet series.

While not directly translatable into interest in continuing education, these figures suggest that there are substantial numbers of subscribers whose interests go well beyond conventional television fare. For example, if 5 percent of a cable system with 5,000 subscribers were to enroll in a cablecast course, that would result in a class of at least 250, which ought to furnish an adequate economic base for such a course. These figures also re-emphasize the need for greater information about the "market" for televised education and for more sophisticated knowledge about cable subscribers. Cable operators, unlike broadcasters, know exactly who their customers are, since they usually are in monthly contact with them for billing purposes. It would certainly be a simple matter to poll the cable subscribers about their interests in participating in educational courses via the cable.

4. *The status of cablecasting.* Because most locally originated cablecasting has been constrained by the limited resources available, it inevitably attracts extremely small audiences. Most origination by cable operators has consisted of inexpensive movies or free promotional films or modest imitations of less expensive broadcast formats, such as talk shows, interviews and local news. Probably the most successful kind of local programming produced by cable systems has been the coverage of high school football and basketball and other local sports events. Occasionally, there has been some lively and innovative programming on public-access channels, but even the most enthusiastic "access" producers have felt that their audiences have been negligible. Part of the problem is that the quality of cablecast programs varies greatly from one hour to the next; another part of the problem is that it is extremely difficult for viewers to find out in advance what programs are going to appear on these channels.

Confirmation of the virtual "invisibility" of cable programming can be found in several Canadian surveys. In 1969, the A.C. Nielson Company did a survey of viewing in Middlesex County, Ontario, where the heavily subscribed cable companies had been offering original programs for several years. The Nielson staff reported that they "were unable to find any viewing of measurable proportions of the locally programmed cable channel." A 1971 study of cablecasting in the same area, conducted by Benjamin D. Singer for the Canadian Department of Communications, found the same problem; but Singer also concluded that "When a special purpose program is to be aired and is well-promoted in advance . . . a special purpose audience will view the program and will gain definite social benefits."*

The use of cable for continuing education should be exactly the kind of programming Singer is describing and his point is well-taken. The experiences with cablecasting to date suggest several requirements for effective use of cable channels:

1. A special promotional effort is necessary to make potential students aware of the existence of non-broadcast educational cable programming. Such a campaign should include both general publicity about the existence of cablecast programming and specific information about individual courses.
2. Ensuring production standards of technical competence is a crucial factor in attracting and holding viewers' attention. Since each individual community and institution is unlikely to be able to afford production of high quality programming, sharing production resources will be vital.
3. The most effective uses of cable for education will probably be those programs and courses designed for specific, well-defined groups within the general population. Cable seems best suited for "narrowcasting," while broadcast television remains the medium of choice for courses of very wide general interest.

5. Lack of interconnection of cable systems. The reach of a cable system is characteristically confined to the boundaries of the political entity (usually a municipal government) which granted the system its franchise. Unfortunately, these boundaries often do not conform to the larger areas served by institutions of higher learning. In California, for example, community college districts are usually county-wide and may cover many municipalities and, hence, many cable systems. Yet the value of offering courses via cable is obviously much greater if the entire college district can be covered. Programming can be "bicycled" from system to system, of course, but this adds considerably to the expense and complexity of offering courses and is likely to be a sufficient deterrent to prevent the organization of the program in the first place.

Clearly, the best time to consider the interconnection of cable systems is before they are built. For example, five cities in Orange County, California, all within the boundaries of the Coast Community College District, have formed a Public Cable Television Authority to study their communications needs and develop a franchise proposal. While the decision has not yet been made whether a single franchise or separate franchises will be granted, the systems will definitely be interconnected for joint uses. The Coast Community College District has been

*Benjamin D. Singer, *Cablecast.* Ottawa: Canadian Department of Communications, Report S-DEC-1, n.d.

an active participant in the Cable Television Authority's planning, since the district wishes to use the system for expanding access to its educational services.

Eventually, satellites will provide the possibility for nation-wide interconnection of cable systems. This will permit the accumulation of substantial audiences, even for specialized programming—just 1 percent of the current 6.5 million cable subscribers is 65,000 homes. A national cable network will undoubtedly be first established for entertainment programming via pay-cable (as in the plan of Hughes Aircraft); but once such a system is created, it should be possible to use it effectively for educational purposes as well. What kinds of educational services would be effective nationally, who would produce the programs, and how would the courses be accredited and supported need further attention. In the more immediate future, modest levels of interconnection are possible and should be explored.

Discussion
Walter S. Baer

Dr. Baer is director of the Aspen Workshop on Uses of the Cable and a consultant to the Communications Policy Program of the Rand Corporation. His Rand publications include *Interactive Television: Prospects for Two-Way Services on Cable* (1971), *Cable Television: A Handbook for Decisionmaking* (1973), and *Cable Television: A Guide to the Technology* (with Carl Pilnick, 1973). At the opening session of the Aspen Workshop conference, Dr. Baer provided a brief update on the status of cable and commented on several other implications of the FCC cable rules.

On March 31st, 1972, a new set of FCC regulations went into effect that changed the rules of the game for cable television in its approach to building systems in the major television markets. Briefly, the rules were a compromise over what kind of television signals cable systems would carry. It was resolved that big-city cable systems could bring in two and perhaps three commercial television stations from other communities. That issue is further complicated, however, by a recent court ruling that copyright payments may be required for these signals. The question of copyright for cable television, both in bringing in commercial broadcasts and pay-TV and also in carrying educational programs, is very much an issue today.

The new regulations also state criteria for awarding franchises and give a set of requirements that cable systems in the 100 largest television markets have to fulfill in terms of channel capacity, channels available for access, and other technical aspects of the system. The first, and probably most important, is that new big-city systems must have at least 20 channels and, furthermore, that for every channel of broadcast television that they carry, they must have at least one channel available for non-broadcast use. This provides most systems today with a considerable amount of channel capacity that they will not be using at the beginning.

The FCC rules also require that three channels must be dedicated for access purposes: One channel for public access, to make television time available to the general public usually on a first-come, first-served basis; a second channel for use by the local government for whatever purposes it deems important; and a third channel available for educational uses; free for at least five years. What happens after five years is not at all clear. In addition to the free channels, new cable systems also have to have other channels available for lease. It's very likely that if educational applications develop, a single channel won't be enough, and the most interesting uses of cable will involve use of these leased channels.

Finally, the FCC rules say that new cable systems must have a *capacity* for two-way communications. Actual two-way services do not have to be offered to subscribers. The two-way requirement is restricted to "non-voice" communications: that is, the ability to send messages back from a subscriber to the control studio at the head end. The subscriber, of course, could be a school as well as an individual at home. Two two-way "capacity" might be satisfied by putting in a system that has amplifier housings in which amplifiers for the return signals can be installed at some later time.

While a telephone line would not, in itself, satisfy the two-way capacity requirement of the FCC, many uses of the two-way communications in cable systems in the near future will use a telephone line for the return link. True interactive cable television is still many years away in most systems. Consequently discussions of educational applications for cable should assume the use of telephone lines or the mails for returning information from individuals at home, rather than the use of two-way cable systems themselves.

Discussion

Barry Zorthian

Mr. Zorthian has a distinguished background in journalism and government service. He is currently president of Time-Life Cable Communications, which owns the Sterling cable system in New York City. He recounted for the conference some of the problems faced by the industry in developing cable systems in the major urban markets.

I speak from the viewpoint of one cable operator facing the unique task of building a system in the inner core city of Manhattan Island. I would hope to bring to you some elements of reality on the prospects and the problems that cable is facing today. I do not want to present a discouraging picture, because I think cable's future is a bright one; but if I had to have a theme, I would adopt a quotation from T. S. Eliot and say to you, "there is a considerable gap between the glow and the reality of the day." I hope cable isn't forever poised on the verge of the future. But there are some dangers of this happening, and I think you ought to be aware of them.

There are four major elements in cable—economics, hardware, regulation and utilization. They obviously interrelate to each other, complement each other and affect each other. The area of economics is one that is somewhat overlooked.

Cable is a commercial business with a profit motive, but a man who is looking for immediate profit in operations is likely to find great disappointment today. Despite the image, cable in operational terms is not making significant money. In fact, the image of great riches in cable is hurting it, because many elements are putting pressures on the cable operator to provide all kinds of services. Money is being made in cable, but it is largely in the stock market or in terms of the buying and selling of franchises and not from operations.

Hardware is also a very real problem, but again the great prospects for the future have tended to be misleading. I'll make a flat statement subject to the drawbacks of all generalizations: There *is* no true two-way equipment available on the shelf for anyone to buy. It exists in prototype; it exists in laboratories; it exists in experimental systems. But if you wanted to build a two-way system today, it can't be done at any price that is at all reasonable. A lot of the black box talk today is not true two-way communication but rather control channels for pay-cable purposes. The price today of truly interactive black boxes is certainly up in the range of $200 per subscriber and could be higher. Obviously, those costs are going to come down; ultimately we are going to have a cheap instrument like the telephone. But today the movement toward those goals is slow. It has great potential, perhaps, in development, but it doesn't exist in real terms today.

Regulation? Cable may well become the most highly regulated industry in the history of our country. There are three tiers of regulation: municipal, state and federal. These regulatory bodies are sometimes in conflict, sometimes in coordination; but there is very little in cable today that is not subject to considerable government control. The smothering of an industry before it even really starts to breathe is a very real danger.

And finally, utilization. How are we going to utilize the great capacity that cable represents? Very little start has been made in that regard, but at this moment the concept of the cable operator tends toward entertainment—toward more of the same, with profit in mind. I remind you that of the top ten TV markets, only New York, Los Angeles and San Francisco have granted cable franchises, and only New York has a major system. If you take the top 50 markets, with 60 percent of the population, the amount of cable is very, very small. A figure of 7 million cable subscribers is misleading, because when it's broken down, it consists largely of 2,000 to 3,000 subscriber systems. The universe of cable is limited at this point, and if you start talking about interconnected cables or core-city cable or, in educational terms, of reaching students and educators, you are not talking about today's capabilities.

Many of the problems cable faces are financial. Costs have become enormous. Today, we construct systems at about $150 per subscriber. If you project 15 million subscribers in the next ten years, the amount of cash required probably is in the billions. While I feel certain that money will be available, venture capital is raising some questions about cable; for as a result of the higher cost of government regulations and the difficulties of large-scale construction in urban areas, cable is becoming more like a utility. The costs are likely to increase, not decrease. And if we're going to get into two-way communication, which I think we inevitably are, we must virtually double the cost.

Cable was supposedly unleashed in 1971. That unleashing has led so far to the approval of about 700 certificates of compliances, virtually all of them in small towns. Any substantial franchise applications, again as a generalization, are being resisted by broadcast interests and are still bogged down in the FCC. When the process of approval is finally underway in earnest, it will lead to expansion; but, today, regulation is restraining cable, not encouraging it.

Other regulatory aspects that are under current review involve pay-cable. Exactly where is that going? It looks as if pay-cable is not going to be permitted free access to the market. There are going to be siphoning rules of various kinds and restrictions on the products that can be used. Again, these restrictions will have a major effect on cable's growth.

Copyright? The bill proposed by Senator McClellan adds at least another potential 5 percent of cost on top of everything else. In an area like Manhattan today, almost 15 percent of the gross disappears into overhead before you open your doors in the morning. Now that's before taxes as well as before the potential copyright fee. Cable has been prepared to pay copyright, but the prices that are involved may be prohibitive. Copyright owners have already started bargaining at 17 percent of gross, and Senator McClellan's 5 percent is regarded by them as an unacceptable possibility. They intend to fight all the way.

Other regulatory aspects constitute further drains: Demands are being imposed by local jursidictions. Several states have set up their own cable supervisory groups, which will take further cable revenues to underwrite their costs. Beyond that, these groups will undoubtedly want to undertake regulation in order to leave their own impact on the industry. There are an awful lot of people nibbling at this somewhat limited piece of cheese. I guess the statement most indicative of the attitude of public officials was New York's Mayor Lindsay telling a group of mayors that "We're sitting on an oil gusher. Our only real problem is to stop the federal government from draining all these revenues away." Andrew Heiskell, Time, Inc.'s chairman, responded with the comment that the comparison was a typical observation about oil by an Easterner who had never heard of a dry well.

Another major instance of stifling regulation is the whole anti-trust issue. In view of all these business problems, there has been a process of consolidation going on in cable. The trend was very active for about two years, during which a number of mergers—the inevitable grouping together of economic units to face up to these enormous financial demands—took place. The Justice Department has stepped in on the last of these actions—the proposed merger between Cox and ATC. That is now in the courts and it is going to go to trial in June. This case can have a very significant influence on the success of cable. The industry has total revenues of 350 million dollars, and the two companies involved in this case would have combined revenues of 30 to 40 million dollars. The biggest cable company—TelePrompTer—has revenues of 460 million. The Department of Justice has said at this point that the ATC-Cox merger presents anti-competitive issues and is going to court to stop it. I don't know what will finally come of this, but it is having a considerably inhibiting effect on the forming of economic units that can face up to financial tasks I've described. There seems to be a philosophy in Washington of holding cable to fragmented, Mama-and-Papa-size operations. If that does happen, much of cable's potential is not going to come about.

Where you draw the line regarding over-concentration of economic power is a very difficult question, I grant; but I suggest that a 30 or 40 million dollar company in a growth industry is not the place to start. Cable is facing this kind of a problem today.

I won't get into utilization in great detail. I do say to you that the movement on the part of the larger cable owners is toward pay-cable as a very essential source of ancillary income to basic subscribers revenues. Now just what form this will take, with what type of payments, with what type of hardware, and all the rest of the key questions, is now in the process of being worked out. In the larger cities at least—and I say this specifically about Manhattan out of personal experience—cable is not going to make it on subscriber fees only. Ancillary income has to be found, and the most obvious source is pay-cable for entertainment, sports and movies. Presumably payment for other things—cultural events at Lincoln Center, informational programs, teaching programs, do-it-yourself programs—will also be received; but essentially, at this point, entertainment is the direction in which we are looking. Now there are other ancillary businesses on the horizon as well: information retrieval, data transmission, retailing, the monitoring of gas meters, burglar systems, etc.—a whole range of uses of the electronic impulse. But those are still down the road. Hardware is hard to come by and is going to be very expensive. And in any case, these possibilities are not going to produce that much revenue at an early date. Also, there are questions as to whether the system will have to act as a common carrier for these purposes. Right now, pay-cable is the one area that is being pursued as a practical prospect, but it is still at a very embryonic stage. There is a great deal of development to come there and regulation is going to be critical.

Other uses of cable—the potential great diversity of programming—are very limited at this point, almost pre-embryonic, if you will. We are about to celebrate in New York our second anniversary of the public-access channels. Public access is being used and being used relatively well, although it is still fairly amateurish, both in technique and equipment. But public access is already creating problems for us and for itself. One is the nature of material—what is the responsibility of the cable operator in terms of control. We're under very real pressures in New York because a few users have turned out to be exhibitionists. There is the whole complex issue of obscenity. Access has not been as active a political forum as one might like. It is being used some in that regard, but it tends to be more an outlet for individuals who range all the way from exhibitionists, to those who have particular axes to grind, to those who simply want to see themselves talking. How many people actually watch public access is difficult to measure, but it's not large. Most of them watch the over-the-air signals; most of them have taken cable in New York because of the improvement of signal or because they want to see professional basketball and hockey.

We are also approaching the second anniversary of the transmission of two special channels for the New York City government. The net result is virtually zero. New York City runs its own UHF television channel and it puts that on its cable channels. Otherwise, it runs some police training films, or it runs an occasional promotional film about New York. The city has its budgetary problems, so it has not put a cent into the preparation of material for cable. Those two channels sit there blank day after day, available for the educators. For instance, New York City might welcome a plan for educational use of those channels, yet it has not received a single proposal.

Other diverse uses of the cable are of limited value. Visual Information Systems has tried channel M for doctors in New York on a commercial basis with very limited success. I think it signed up only a couple hundred doctor subscribers, and the system has just about gone off. We've looked at a number of other areas—retail selling by cable, data retrieval for one of the banks, various other possibilities. They're going to come through in due time but it's moving very slowly and the realities of paying current bills is certainly delaying us

I am painting a black picture deliberately in order to try to provide balance for the very frequent misconceptions and illusions about how fast cable can go. I have lost none of my enthusiasm for the eventual potential of cable. I think it is all that we've said it is. But there are enormous problems that have to be recognized, and they're going to get solved slower than anyone anticipates. If the educational world is going to sit and wait for the cable operators to come to them and to provide the where-with-all to undertake education through cable, they have a long wait coming. The cable operator today is trying to establish a business. His stocks are depressed; his profits, if they exist at all, tend to be somewhat artificial because of the ways of financing. He has serious problems in his operation. And while he will be public-spirited and responsive, initiatives in the special uses of cable, for education or any other purpose, must come from the outside.

I should add one footnote to my comments to save us some confusion. There are three cable industries growing, and it helps to keep in mind the differences. One is the traditional community television service—remote communities, small numbers of subscribers. They've made their basic investment, and they don't want to hear about public access or pay-cable. They are a going operation—really a transmission service. Another cable industry is what I call cable television, which is probably the markets 50 to 100—the second-, third- and fourth-size cities. Distant signals have an appeal here. You can undertake some origination; but primarily you're bringing more over-the-air television programming to the subscriber, and that has pretty good potential profit—a penetration of up to 60 percent because of this extra programming.

The third cable industry is what I would call cable communications—a whole new industry, largely headed for the highly populated urban centers. Manhattan is a forerunner. When it is all built, it is going to be a true communications system. The economic basis for the liability, and so on, are still question marks that have to be worked out, but we have gone from community antennas to cable television to cable communications. I think these differences might be helpful to keep in mind in talking about some of the problems.

Discussion

W. Bowman Cutter

Mr. Cutter is executive director of the Cable Television Information Center, established in Washington, D.C., in 1972 to provide assistance to municipal officials engaged in formulating and granting cable franchises for their communities. While recognizing the reality of the problems described by Barry Zorthian, he gave a more optimistic appraisal of cable's immediate future.

It may surprise you that I don't have considerable disagreements with Barry Zorthian's conclusions. I think that his points were perhaps more pessimistic because he's operating out of New York City. Let me make four comments in four areas, three of which may tend to somewhat moderate Barry's pessimism, and the fourth to emphasize it.

In terms of the technology, I think that the marginal system is considerably different from the average system today. The average system that exists across the country has only 9 to 12 channels and no two-way capacity, provides few services, is not interconnected with other systems, is not in a large urban center, and has a high penetration rate based largely on people's attempt to get better television reception. The marginal system, the one being built and planned today, is generally being planned for considerably larger amounts of subscribers. They will have at least 20 channels, and they are being built in a manner that is going to permit expansion of channel capacity. They're being planned with some two-way capability at the start. Because they're in larger communities than in the past, consideration is being given to certain forms of switching abilities as well. Regional cable networks, now almost entirely limited to systems owned by one operator, are being established, and the operators themselves are emphasizing cablecasting and local programming. So there is some reason to say that the systems that are being planned and built today are quite different in terms of capabilities than the ones that now exist.

In terms of movement, my own sense is that cable is moving a lot faster than it was six months, eight months, a year ago. We don't, in our work, ever run into a community today that doesn't have cable applications on hand and isn't, in fact, seriously considering it. I would agree with Barry that the larger the size of the market, the less likely that this is so. The last systems to be operating are going to be in the top ten television markets. Below that, though, there's considerable activity. The industry complains about the delay that is involved in the consideration of alternatives by municipalities. Certainly, there is ample opportunity for frustration in the delays and the time it seems to take to go from the occurrence of cable as an idea to the franchising and operating of the system. However, my own sense is that there is very considerable movement in the communities below the top 20 television markets in cable today.

In terms of economics, I think that Barry's optimism has been skewed by the New York experience, which everyone will admit is very, very tough. New York is the prime case where signal importation, or at least the signals being allowed to be imported by the FCC, are irrelevant to economics. New York does not need another NBC or CBS. This is true, to a considerable degree, in most of the top 50 markets. My own sense is that the signal importation that the FCC allows is going to have, at best, a marginal impact on cable economics. My other sense, though, is somewhat more optimistic. I think that the systems in the top 50 to 100 markets are going to bring a return of somewhere around 10 to 15 percent on equity over a ten-year period, given some assumptions about franchise durations and terminations. Cable, at the moment, is a business in which the operator accepts a risk with a moderate rate of return for the chance to realize all of these initial services. That means it is a high risk business. But I would be more optimistic than Barry about economics.

In terms of the usage, I am more pessimistic. Except for New York, Reading, Pennsylvania, and Orlando, Florida, there isn't a significant public-access operation in the country. The municipal and educational channels are not being used. There is very little planning or thought being given to many of the cable possibilities. Most of the kinds of public programming that are occurring are part of an operator's local-origination efforts. There is public information programming— the Officer Friendly-type stuff—rather than anything that delivers public service or education. There is some planning, of course, but when you look around for the evidence of action, you really see very, very little.

The Obstacles to
Television-Supported Continuing Education

4

From the educational side, real obstacles still stand in the path of the success-ful use of cable for continuing education. The most serious of these obstacles are

1. faculty resistance;
2. legal and copyright problems;
3. pricing inequities;
4. lack of an effective information and dissemination network;
5. lack of information on the "market" for non-traditional education;
6. shortage of qualified specialists;
7. shortage of money.

1. *Faculty resistance.* Given the present institutional structure of post-second-ary education, faculty members often resist or refuse to accept television as an element in the instructional process. Although some of this resistance is based on ignorance or inflexibility or false premises, other concerns are very real, includ-ing the professor's traditional unwillingness to allow others to intrude into a course, the belief that televised courses do not measure up to established academ-ic standards, and the fear of technological displacement.

There is good evidence that post-secondary level faculty balk at adopting "canned" television courses because they consider such courses an intrusion on their independence and individuality as teachers. For example, of the several highly successful television-based courses offered by the Southern California conat this writing only one has been used—and only one time—by another institution. Likewise, the Chicago TV College courses have found little use elsewhere, despite their availability through the Great Plains National ITV Library.

Faculty members expect to be tutors and guides as well as transmitters of information; and we also expect them to give something of their own unique qualities and expertise. Otherwise, learners could rely exclusively on textbooks. It is understandable that professors balk at the notion of adopting someone else's televised course while reducing themselves to secondary roles.

The solution to this obstacle might be found in the analogous situation of readings, books, or anthologies. Faculty members now make extensive use of readings from the works of others in conventional courses, but each of them usually guards jealously his right to select and to sequence such readings to fit into his own concept of the course and his assessment of his students. The television analogy is obvious. If faculty members preparing televised courses were able to draw upon taped courses prepared elsewhere, or on high-quality single concept modules of varying length, some of the faculty resistance would certainly be reduced. In addition, the cost of tailoring locally acceptable courses would be reduced. With proper technical support, each institution (or faculty member) could devise its own courses employing the best units from work done elsewhere, arranged and bridged together with local material in a local production facility. It seems likely that the progress of post-secondary instructional television is going to be strongly dependent on the easy availability of course modules rather than on complete sequences or courses. A mechanism for facilitating this process is discussed below under point 4, the topic of dissemination.

The second inhibitor to faculty acceptance of television is skepticism of the medium as an effective teaching tool. The failure of available technology to make much penetration into post-secondary education despite 20 years of substantial support and ballyhoo has quite naturally raised doubts and strengthened the hands of the confirmed doubters. Part of the remedy, clearly, is to inform faculties about the many isolated successes that have been achieved; for the evidence is overwhelming that students learn as well in a well-designed television-based course as in the conventional alternate. The point is that television instruction can be dull or shoddy, just as can classroom teaching. But neither has to be.

Of equal, or even greater, importance in convincing faculty of the effectiveness of television is exposing them to the unfamiliar technology. What is unfamiliar is often perceived as threatening; and if television is to be accepted as an integral part of the educational system, faculty members must begin to feel as comfortable in a television studio as they now do in a classroom. This task will be neither quick nor simple, but it can be accomplished only by actually involving teachers—and administrators—in the planning and creation of televised materials.

The final inhibitor to faculty acceptance of television has to do with whether television will lead to expanded enrollment, or whether it will be a substitute for campus courses and will displace existing faculty. Television proponents have been quick to point out that successful educational offerings on television have sortium, appealed to *new* students, even attracting many of them into conventional programs. But perhaps they have been too quick with their reassurances; for there are already evidences of displacement. A Colorado State University televised accounting course has permitted a faculty reduction of seven, according to officials there. And a new astronomy course in the Southern California Consortium coincided with a reduction in on-campus enrollments at the originating college and led to cancellation of three sections of the regular course. There is, of course, balancing anecdotal evidence. On another campus of the same consortium, introduction of a televised course in health education coincided with increased on-campus enrollment in the same course.

So long as televised efforts continue to concentrate on peripheral or elective courses and not the "bread and butter" core courses, and so long as TV enrollments are a small fraction of the total enrollment of a school (as in the case of Chicago TV College), the displacement effect should be negligible. Nevertheless, evidences of displacement will not be lost on dubious faculty members or on union officials, and the topic of displacement should not to be taken lightly or treated deceptively.* Rather, it seems wiser to deal directly with the issue and to seek offsets, such as increasing the time off from regular duties for preparation of televised courses, or providing for additional faculty compensation or a share of royalties from TV courses sold to other institutions.

2. *Legal and copyright problems.* In a number of instances, problems of ownership, content control, royalties and related legal matters have stood in the way of obtaining wider use of televised material in education. However, most such problems can be avoided through careful advance planning. Institutions that have pioneered in the development of college-level television material have learned to use a variety of arrangements to get material produced and on the air. Typical is the Southern California Consortium, whose executive director recommended the following basic principles to avoid legal problems:†

> *1. Whatever the task, whether an arrangement with a faculty member to develop a course or an agreement with an external production facility, specify the rights and expectations of all parties through a contract, even if some services are provided gratis. What starts out as a modest cooperative experiment may become a valuable product, and after-the-fact squabbling resulting from unclear understandings may be both unpleasant and costly to all concerned.*
> *2. The simplest approach to ownership and copyright is to pay the faculty*

---

*The displacement problem can take another form that concerns faculties—fear that expenditures for televised education, especially the heavy expenditures required for course production, will be taken out of the existing budget and will force cuts in personnel and services.

†Speech by August DeJong at a conference on Open Circuit Instructional Television, co-sponsored by the California Community Colleges Chancellor's Office and the California Junior College Association. Burlingame, California, January 11, 1973.

member a fixed fee for his services and assign the copyright to the employing institution.

3. When there is a choice between production facilities of comparable quality, select the facility in which complications are least—for example, the facility that is not under a union contract, so that faculty "performers" are not required to join the artists' union; or the facility where ownership rights to the finished product are not in question but rest with the educational institution. Freedom from legal complications may outweight short-run cost savings.

4. Obtain capable legal counsel in advance and abide by it. Public institutions can usually rely on government counsel.

3. *Pricing inequities.* Televised courses are so new that tuition and fee policies are not yet well-established. Some states provide public institutions with smaller reimbursements for televised courses than for on-campus courses. The assumption is that televised courses are less costly to the institution, which may ultimately be the case, although costs in the initial stages of development and production are generally higher. Other states require public colleges to charge fees equal to the incremental cost of off-campus instruction for TV and other external students, while on-campus study is so highly subsidized that it is certainly cheaper and often free.

The best solution to these discrepancies is, of course, to assess the same charges and fees for all forms of instruction. All are supposed to be of the same quality and value; they should cost the same amount. There is no reasonable justification for giving in effect second-class status to TV or any other external students. This solution is a matter for legislative action in most states.

4. *Lack of an information and dissemination network.* All of the institutions and agencies that produce material for television or acquire it for libraries or learning centers acknowledge that gathering information on what is available or in-production is a haphazard—and therefore inefficient and costly—process. This absence of systematic dissemination mechanisms often thwarts adoption of televised material by educational institutions. In particular, the post-secondary institutions are not being served by existing dissemination organizations. The Great Plains Library and the National Instructional Television Center, among others, distribute information about available material as well as tapes and films, but they are primarily concerned with the pre-college level. Others, such as the Nebraska Educational Television Council for Higher Education, serve only local institutions.

There is an urgent need for a national agency, or several closely linked regional agencies, to facilitate the production and shared use of televised materials in post-secondary education. The establishment of such a dissemination and facilitation network appears essential if television is to become an important element in continuing and post-secondary education. The report of the Carnegie Commission on Higher Education, *The Fourth Revolution,* proposes establishment of several regional "cooperative learning-technology centers," each of which would include a production unit, a library resource unit, a distribution unit and a computing unit. Each would require an initial capital investment of $35 million and an annual operating expense of $150 million.*

Certainly, a more modestly scaled plan, concentrating on the first and third functions proposed for the Carnegie Commission's centers, is within closer reach and could begin to fulfill the immediate needs of television-supported education. The range of tasks that these more modest centers would undertake includes:

1. Collecting and assessing videotaped materials, informing institutions about these materials, and distributing the materials. The assessment—a critical review of materials and determination of the audiences and situations for which they would be useful—is an especially essential step. The results of such assessments would be published for potential users, and the distribution arrangements made through the centers or through commercial distributors. Modules of specialized materials for the construction of local courses should also be included in this assessment/distribution process. These functions are similar to thsoe successfully performed now on a pre-college level by centers like the Great Plains National ITV Library (Lincoln, Nebraska) and the National Instructional Television Center (Bloomington, Indiana).

2. Keeping abreast of the production plans and on-going efforts of colleges and consortia and informing others of these activities through conferences, regular publications and other media. This service could eliminate much of the re-duplication of effort that now seems to be occurring in the production and planning of various institutions. This service might be especially useful in improving production efforts through the sharing of ideas and materials.

3. Providing a field service that would serve as a catalyst for local production, for utilization of existing materials in the creation of local courses, for encouraging the formation of consortia, and for bringing educational institutions together with both cable operators and broadcasters.

4. Providing counsel to institutions on organizational, legal, technical and production problems.

5. Producing or commissioning the production of modules, course segments or courses, whenever a clear need exists and the initiative is not forthcoming from educational institutions.

5. *Lack of information on the "market" for non-traditional education.* Another barrier to intelligent growth of television-supported continuing education is the lack of information about what potential students want to study. Most offerings to date have been selected by hunch, or based on the proven merits of a charismatic teacher, or taken from the standard core curriculum. The first meth-

---

*Carnegie Commission on Higher Education, *The Fourth Revolution—Instructional Technology in Higher Education.* New York: McGraw-Hill Book Company, 1972.

od appears effective but very limited—there are only a few sure-fire topics, such as ecology and ethnic studies, and they can change very quickly. The second method—reliance on professional charm—means less as we progress beyond the "talking head" in televised courses to material that makes full use of the power of the medium. The third method—offering core courses—is undoubtedly the most sound and will become a requirement as more students enroll in televised programs with the intent of earning degrees. Thus far, however, many institutions have avoided giving such courses over television in order to sidestep faculty resistance and fears of displacement. We actually know very little about public demand for televised courses, especially in the career-oriented areas and in self-help and personal-development subjects. A few limited surveys have been conducted by questionnaire and interview, but they generally have not been followed up with course offerings. Consequently, we have insufficient experience to translate stated interest into actual enrollments.

6. *Shortage of qualified specialists.* Institutions sponsoring televised offerings need qualified media specialists to design and operate the programs; but few such specialists are on the scene today, and there are even fewer systematic arrangements for training new ones. A need for organized training programs is apparent.

The Carnegie Commission's *The Fourth Revolution* urges "that some institutions of higher learning arrange now for the introduction of instruction designed to train the new specialists who will have new career opportunities in higher education in the coming decades." The existing departments and schools of communications, which now concentrate on training students for commercial broadcast television production, could profitably offer specialized training to their students for working with faculty in the design and production of television-based educational materials. And since much of the technique of mounting effective televised instruction can best be learned through experience, there is also merit in founding and supporting clinical training centers in institutions already successfully using television. Internships and short-term workshops would permit practitioners to transfer their knowledge and skills to apprentices. Modest external support could facilitate such activities and assure the supply of specialists needed for television-supported education.

7. *Shortage of money.* Although listed last, this is among the most fundamental issues to be faced by educational television. The problem of money is two-pronged: first, establishing reliable estimates of the cost of producing effective television-based educational programs, and, second, finding sources of support for the development of new programs and for continued support of those which are successful. The cost of producing televised courses can and does vary widely. At the most austere level, it is possible to videotape classroom instruction in black and white with simple equipment at a cost of $25-$100 per hour. These tapes are not of broadcast quality but are technically adequate for cablecasting. However, in the absence of an unusually charismatic teacher, such programming is unlikely to attract and hold viewer attention for long. At the other

end of the cost scale are the elaborately produced, subtly edited color productions which may approach commercial network productions in cost. For example, "Sesame Street" cost more than $30,000 per hour to produce, as did the cultural anthropology course produced by the Coast Community Colleges (the costs included sending film crews to Europe and the Middle East).

Most courses involving moderately sophisticated production should fall in the middle range of approximately $3,000-$5,000 per hour. H. S. Dordick's "Business Plan Edu-Cable"* has estimated that course production for a proposed "Edu-Cable" instructional service would vary from $300 per hour for "simple" unedited tapes to $1,200 per hour for more sophisticated color production. Other experience suggests that these estimates are somewhat low. According to a recent Rand report, the cost for production of courses by the Chicago TV College in 1972-73 averaged $3,900 per hour, and the courses produced by the Bavarian Telekolleg in Germany in 1971 averaged $5,250 per hour.† The cost of a typical Southern California Consortium television course is approximately $4,500 per hour, and Stuart Cooney, director of the Northern California ITV Consortium, estimates that $3,500 per hour is a minimum for producing good quality pre-recorded programs.†† (See Table 3 for a summary of these costs.)

Table 3. Summary of Costs
for Production of Televised Courses

Description	Cost per hour
Simple black and white taped instruction	$25-100
Edu-Cable estimate	$300-1,200
Coast Colleges' psychology course	$3,300
No. California Consortium estimate	$3,500
Chicago TV College	$3,900
Bavarian Telekolleg	$4,500
"Sesame Street"	$31,200-35,400
Coast Colleges' cultural anthropology course	$33,000

Of course, the larger the total audience for a televised course, the greater the production expense that can be justified. The Rand report cited above indicates

---

*A hypothetical model for a profit-making educational service to be offered via pay-cable channels. See Part II, p. 119.

†Rudy Bretz, *Three Models for Home-Based Instructional Systems Using Television.* Santa Monica: Rand Report R-1089-USOE/MF, October 1972.

††Stuart Cooney, "A Three Year Plan." Northern California Regional Instructional Television Consortium, California State University at Sonoma, December 15, 1972, mimeographed.

that although the cost per hour of producing "Sesame Street" is nearly 10 times greater than that of the Chicago TV College courses, the cost per viewer is 25 times greater for the Chicago TV College! It should also be noted that repeated use of taped materials will permit costs to be amortized over several showings, and some costs may also be recovered through the sale or rental of materials to other institutions. Finally, it is important to keep in mind that production costs are only one component of the financial requirements for a television-supported course. For an effective course, the cost of supplementary services—promotion, preparation of written materials, provision for faculty-student and student-student contact, and mechanisms for evaluation or feedback—may equal or surpass the expense of the television production.

The second financial issue to be faced by television-supported education is that of finding sources of support. Even though televised instruction promises to be a cost-saver in the long-run, new and substantial funds are needed for the initial development of the programs. Producing an inventory of new courses and course modules will be costly, but such a backlog of material will also have usefulness for many years. Thus, building these resources should be looked upon as a capital investment, and grants or appropriations for such purposes should be considered apart from ordinary operating funds. Later updating of material can probably be done out of operating budgets or out of funds set aside from the revenues that good courses and modules can generate.

This removal of early production investments from operating budgets can go a long way toward relieving faculty fears of budget competition. Ultimately, of course, televised courses will have to compete with other demands for the instructional dollar, but new funds will be needed during the initial period of program development. Legislative bodies and foundations must be made aware of this distinction between "start-up" investments and operating support. To reiterate, once the major production expenses of "start-up" are met, the regular operating budgets of educational institutions should be expected to cover the cost of operational use of televised courses, with rental and sale fees accumulated for subsequent revision of the programs or for new productions.

Much of the past support for television-supported instruction has come from funds intended for innovative programs. Short-term foundation grants, state experimental funds, and research and development money from various federal sources (U.S. Office of Education, National Science Foundation, and possibly the new National Center for Educational Technology) can be looked to for support in the coming years. But once television-based continuing education courses emerge from the experimental phase, additional sums will be required to build the necessary backlog of materials for a comprehensive program. If a total of say 500 post-secondary and continuing education courses are to be provided with televised support materials at a production cost of $50,000 to $100,000 for each course, we are looking at an initial investment of $25 to $50 million over the next five to ten years.

State and local educational authorities would seem to be the obvious sources for such investments, since they stand to benefit directly from advances in educational productivity. However, there are some problems with state and local funding. One problem is that reliance on the states may result in needless duplication of effort in some areas and gaps in others. Furthermore, the amounts required are substantial, and this financial burden would inevitably fall on just a few of the larger states. A strong case can therefore be made for support from the federal level.

The Future of Cablecast Continuing Education

5

This is a time of great ferment in education. The campus turmoil of the 1960s left a legacy of unanswered questions about the role of education in our society. The financial crisis being felt by both local school districts and the most prestigious universities suggests the need for a re-examination of the costs and the benefits educational institutions are providing. In addition, the communications revolution, of which the cable is a part, is rapidly breaking down the dependence of education on time and place.

These developments are creating a rich array of quests and programs for changing existing institutions and creating new institutions to expand access to education. We may be seeing the first stages of a more comprehensive educational system for our society—a system designed to provide general and specialized educational opportunities on demand throughout an individual's lifetime. This chapter will explore these possibilities, examining the institutions—old and new, educational and corporate—that will play a role in bringing this system into being.

Existing colleges and universities. The Commission on Non-Traditional Study reports that nearly one-half of the post-secondary educational institutions they surveyed currently offer one or more non-traditional programs. Approximately one-third of these programs appear to the commission to be truly innovative. These findings suggest that there is a growing receptivity to change in colleges and universities but that the change is often moderated by faculty resistance and institutional constraints. Existing institutions have great investments in their

75

physical facilities and they have built powerful traditions around full-time residential study. Still, as the costs of higher education continue to increase, and as the pool of young candidates for college diminishes, these institutions will feel the growing pressure for them to reach out to new audiences, and the non-traditional programs will become truly new and innovative.

The community colleges seem best-suited to take the lead in developing programs of television-based extramural education. These colleges were designed to serve the needs of entire communities; their faculties are experienced in dealing with a wide range of student abilities and interests; and both the administrations and teachers are less burdened with tradition and more willing to use courses produced elsewhere. The Newman Commission found that the community colleges are now "the leading edge of the effort to extend opportunity for education beyond the elite to all citizens." Unfortunately, community colleges, though the fastest growing segment of higher education, are not spread evenly across the country. Six states—California, Florida, Illinois, Michigan, New York, and Texas—account for two-thirds of all community colleges, and California alone for one-third.

The Newman Commission also found evidence of a "discouraging scenario" being acted out among these community colleges. These innovative, community-based institutions are transformed into "amorphous, bland, increasingly large, increasingly state-dominated, two-year institutions which serve a number of interests other than that of their students." If this trend continues, the commission warns, we may see "the conversion of promising new institutions into glorified high schools or lower-division appendages or the four-year institutions."* However, some encouraging counter-trends can still be found. A recent issue of the *Journal of the American Association of Community and Junior Colleges* (November 1972) was devoted to cable and television-based education and was the first issue in memory to sell out almost immediately. Similarly, a survey reported by the Newman Commission revealed that community college faculty members generally favored increases in occupational programs, community services and adult education rather than increases in lower-division academic programs.

There are also some hopeful signs of activity among four-year institutions. Course materials from Britain's Open University are currently being tested at four American universities—Rutgers, University of Maryland, University of Houston, and California State University at San Diego.† A new consortium of state colleges in Northern California are undertaking some imaginative experiments in using television for continuing education.†† And this past fall, the prestigious American Council on Education issued a special report recommending that "colleges and

---

*Frank Newman *et al.,* pp. 58-59 (see earlier footnote, p. 10).

†Fred Nelson, "The Open University in the United States." *The College Board Review,* No. 85, Fall 1972, pp. 11-14.

††See Part II, p.111, for a fuller description of the consortium.

universities include, as a formal element in all planning, a policy of giving adequate and independent attention to the needs of their adult . . . students," which
would include "the imaginative development of technology as a growing element
in educational programs."*

Even those private institutions which do not engage directly in extramural
education will have contributions to make. Schools like Stanford, Harvard, MIT,
and Cornell should continue to serve as important sources of research and expertise in such areas as communications policy and technology development and
basic educational theory. Schools or departments of communications should also
be helpful to training the manpower necessary for television-based education.

New institutions of higher education. A major reason for the success of the
Open University was the fact that it was a newly created, wholly autonomous
institution devoted solely to providing extramural college-level education leading to a degree. It was unencumbered by previous traditions and did not have
to cope with competing claims of on-campus instruction, since there was no
campus. Furthermore, it had to offer a full curriculum; the selection of courses
for the curriculum was set by the requirements of a college degree.

There are already a number of similarly campus-free institutions in this country, including the University Without Walls (a project of the Union for Experimenting Colleges and Universities based at Antioch College, Yellow Springs,
Ohio), the Minnesota Metropolitan State College, and New York's new Empire
State College. These schools do not provide direct instruction, however, but are
essentially counseling, examining and accrediting institutions for students studying independently. Several states, including New York, also offer credit by examination through agencies which perform only this function. Closer to the Open
University model is the State University of Nebraska (S-U-N), which is currently
being developed with support from the U.S. Office of Education. S-U-N will
offer its courses statewide via the interconnected Nebraska ETV Network.
Courses are being prepared in two areas—psychology and accounting— which
proved most popular in a survey conducted in 1972 in Nebraska. Eventually,
S-U-N hopes to include several surrounding states and offer a complete television-
based curriculum for the first two years of college.

For the more distant future, satellite interconnection of cable systems and
widespread home use of video cassette equipment may lead to the creation of
new national or international institutions devoted to television-based continuing
education. During the next decade, however, the leadership in this field will remain at the local, state or perhaps regional level.

Private enterprise. Stanley Moses' figures† indicate that the fastest growing

---

*Higher Education and the Adult Student," *A.C.E. Special Report.* Washington: American
Council on Education, October 25, 1972.

†See Chapter 1, p. 8.

component of continuing education is the proprietary schools. He projects that their enrollments will nearly double—from 9.6 to 18.1 million—in the period from 1970 to 1975. Although the quality of these schools varies widely, their rapid growth suggests their success in providing practical and intensive training, primarily in vocational areas. Most of these enterprises are wholly consumer-supported.

The proprietary schools have made little use of broadcast television for instruction, because thus far it has not been possible to limit access to paying students. The development of restricted pay-cable channels should offer an attractive new means for offering educational courses on a commercial basis. Edu-Cable, a commercial model described in Part II, would lease pay-cable channels and distribute courses developed and produced by colleges and universities. The proposed Hughes Aircraft satellite would have a somewhat similar plan, in that one of its eight subscription channels for cable systems would be devoted to instruction in cultural arts and crafts activities.

Another model of privately supported cable education is provided by Community Medical Cablecasting. CMC provides biweekly programs of continuing medical education to physicians reached by twelve eastern CATV systems. The programming is provided free of charge over the leased cable channels and is paid for by sponsoring pharmaceutical companies, which use CMC as an advertising medium. Access to these programs is restricted by use of non-standard channels requiring special converters supplied to particpating physicians.

Video cassettes provide a different medium for distributing proprietary instruction. Time-Life Video, for example, today sells a series of cassettes on speed reading taught by Dick Cavett. The course is also offered in New York City at a center to which customers can come and watch the programs at their convenience. Many other companies are eagerly eyeing this potentially vast market, and it seems inevitable that this and other consumer- and sponsor-supported televised education will continue to expand. At least one large commercial company is presently exploring a grand design which would combine cable and broadcast television stations, satellites, and home video cassettes to provide instruction at a profit for everyone from pre-schoolers to retirees. If a voucher system ever were adopted as a major means of educational support, proprietary education would grow even faster; and these proprietary institutions, which pay close attention to the practical value of their instruction and its cost to the consumer, would offer serious competition to traditional educational institutions.

Broadcast television stations. The Sunrise Semester has been a feature of commercial broadcast television since the 1950s, and public television has had its mission of instructional programming for in-school pre-secondary use for almost as long. But for post-secondary and adult education there has been little on broadcast television until very recently. In places like Chicago, Los Angeles and Baltimore, college credit courses are now offered over PTV, and a new high school equivalency program is being developed by the Kentucky Educational TV Network.

The more than 100 local public-television licensees are logical candidates to provide facilities and personnel for production of continuing education courses, and on the national level, the new management of the Corporation for Public Broadcasting has announced its intention to give increased support for cultural and educational programming. As "Sesame Street" and "The Electric Company" have shown, national public television can be instrumental in dealing with clearly identified nation-wide educational needs through imaginative, well-funded projects. The creation of an adult "Sesame Street"* would contribute greatly to demonstrating television's important future role in continuing education. In countries such as England, Japan and Germany, publicly supported television already plays a well-established role in the dissemination of vocational and academic education for adults.

Although this is a difficult period for public television, both politically and financially, it is the proper time for us to assert a claim for continuing education as a major national responsibility for American public television.

Cable industry. The cable industry has been largely preoccupied in recent years with winning franchises and building systems. Despite much rhetoric—most of it from outside the industry—little attention has been given to developing new forms of programming and services for cable. The cable industry will inevitably play a role in implementing these services, so some real commitment of people and funds for educational program development would seem a worthwhile investment. The larger multiple-system operators, in particular, might begin by articulating a strong corporate policy to cooperate fully with local educational institutions. Then they should go one step further and implement this policy in their operating systems; for in many cases, cable operators will have to take the lead in developing contacts with local educators, encouraging the formation of educational consortia to use cable channels, and providing facilities, equipment and production advice. Cable operator initiative may be all that is necessary to catalyze action from local educational institutions.

Similarly, the Cable Television Information Center and other non-commercial groups have concentrated their past efforts on franchising and regulation of cable. While this may be of highest priority today, the real test of cable's value will come after the franchise is granted and a system constructed. Thus, the uses of cable television—of which education may well be the most important— should receive increased attention from those concerned with the development of cable and related communications technologies.

Today the gap between the promise and the reality of cable remains great. It is clear that operators cannot supply all the programming and services which the cable can carry and which will be needed to make cable viable in the country's

---

*The Children's Television Workshop is, in fact, proposing a series of 26 one-hour programs on health for adults and teenagers, to be produced for the 1974-75 season. See William Kobin, "A Proposal for Twenty-Six One-Hour Television Programs on Health," Future Works Division of the Children's Television Workshop, November 1972, Mimeographed.

urban centers. If and when cable is made a common carrier (as a forthcoming Cabinet-level report apparently will recommend), the industry will be wholly dependent on outside program sources to fill its channels.

From the standpoint of both the cable operator and the educator, a working partnership between them offers many exciting possibilities. But the obstacles to be overcome are neither few nor simple. Cable systems have not been built with the needs of education in mind, nor have educators proved eager to explore the potential of new technologies for increasing their effectiveness. Whether or not traditional educational institutions can respond adequately to the challenge of devising the means to meet new educational needs remains to be seen. Perhaps new institutions—certainly new institutional arrangements—are needed. In some cases, the cable industry will have to take greater initiative in stimulating interest in the services it has to offer. Although the first small steps toward a partnership have been taken, few operational successes have yet been achieved. A greater effort on both sides could result in significantly increasing access to education as well as helping cable to realize its full potential.

Discussion

A Final Wrap-Up by the Conference Participants

After three days of sustained discussions of individual projects and specific proposals regarding the cable and continuing education, the final session of the Aspen Workshop conference offered each participant the opportunity to reflect on what had been accomplished in the discussion. The participants also spoke about other topics which, they felt, needed attention or further discussion.

Douglass Cater*

We all feel a certain state of inconclusiveness, but mapping out the future is always disconcerting. The difficulty of trying to figure out whether there is a role for reason or for reasonable men and women is particularly severe in an amorphous world. Trying to put the two elephants of communication and education together in a brief time is a cumbersome business.

I think some of us wish we had done a better job in defining what we mean by continuing education, and yet I have the feeling that if we had come up with a neat definition, the world would not necessarily pay heed to it. It will be what various pressures and demands make it turn out to be. We all feel that cable has an uncertain destiny in this business. I wish we had had more time to talk about the virtues and vices of competing modes of communication.

We might, for example, have discussed Peter Goldmark's plan to make maximum use of midnight and early-morning broadcast time to transmit courses to home video cassette recorders leased to the home-owner. The user could then re-play them at his own convenience. Broadcast stations presently have a reach that far exceeds the cable in the country, and most of them lay unused in the off-hours. It may very well be that, if at all economically feasible, cassettes are going to run a hard competition to cablecasting.

As one looks at this whole thing, one's inclination is to let a thousand flowers

*For affiliations/background of the participants, see list, p. vii.

bloom. Let's let the free world of the marketplace determine it. Yet we know
that public policy is not going to allow the most free type of competition. Thus,
certain strategies and certain guidelines have to be worked out by reasonable
men and women, or else public policy will have a crippling rather than a constructive effect.

However, if we do have a policy that is letting at least a hundred flowers bloom,
if not a thousand, what do we really mean when we say we've got to have quality
control? How do we do it? We certainly don't want to turn over continuing education exclusively to the traditional educators who would impose faulty determinants. That would be the kiss of death. What do we mean by quality control
other than the quality control at the market place? Presumably a student won't
pay for something unless he thinks it's worth it. Is that the most we mean or do
we mean more?

That leads to my final question: How hard a national strategy do we want?
Do we want something as firm as an American Open University, or perhaps a national accrediting institution that can put a Good Housekeeping Seal of Approval
on certain types of local or regional programs? Or is even this, at present, much
too hard a national strategy? Certainly, I don't think that anybody would come
out of this conference thinking that we are ready to create a national Open University in the British mode which actually gets into programming. Those are my
questions and I think that we need to provoke further thought about them.

I do come out of this meeting with two convictions. One is that there is an
urgent need for new entrepreneurs. How do we invent the pioneers and entrepreneurs—Joan Cooneys and the Jack McBrides? That should be a continuing question for public policy, because the future is going to be shaped by the people
who put it all together with enough passion to get the money and make it go. This
is not a very brilliant conclusion, but public policy ought to be prepared to encourage this in both the commercial and the non-profit world. It would be helpful, for example, for non-profit education to have some new entrepreneurs of the
type that built the great universities in the past decades—men who know how to
play in the world of politics and also in the world of finance and get these institutions or these organizations built.

My second conviction is that, as we move into continuing education, we need
to search out new combinations of commercial and non-profit. These two worlds
do not have to be as separate and distinct as they have been.

Robert Filep

Here are some of my continuing concerns. A preamble is needed to describe
the potential of cable for continuing education. This statement has to be placed

in the context of some of the group's earlier observations and might include the
following:

Contrasted to open-broadcast television, cable has a potential that can provide
a positive image of human behavior or transmit the cultural heritage without the
influence of a whole series of commercials that say the human condition is bad,
requires a wide range of medications, and always suffers sleepless nights and gas-
tric upsets. Cable can also proceed with an uplifting spiritual quality that deals
with the potential and best aspects of the individual and not the violent aspects
of human behavior.

But the greatest achievement cable and continuing education could accomplish is to bring about greater individualization of learning. We don't necessarily
need "canned" materials on a continuing basis. I've heard very little or no discussion about how to involve the people interested in continuing education; that is
to say, encouraging people to come into the studio, holding panel discussions
about the work ethic, etc. The thrust of the whole dialogue during the past three
days has been, "What do we have in the "can" that we can put on the tube that
goes out on the cable?"

Another point. You all remember "The Music Man," I'm sure. One sequence
goes, "You've gotta know the territory." I say this to both of the "service industry" groups—the cable operators and the educators—we have to know the territory, both ways.

And another point. I talked about an integrated service approach yesterday.
I'd like to stress that we need an integrated media approach as well. This is basically what Doug Cater was suggesting when he said that we all should look at
cable in relation to satellites and open broadcast televison. And Shaf Nader stated
a beautiful phrase when he said "we should concern ourselves with the robust
development of the communications technology." That's what is happening, and
cable has to fulfill its rightful role and find its place. In the Rocky Mountain
Satellite Project, for instance, the National Center for Educational Technology
is hoping to have at least one cable hook-up in this experiment to see how it relates to the delivery of educational and health services by satellite. If you're interested, you ought to seek out the Rocky Mountain staff, to see how that's
being done and how you might aid and abet that activity.

Genevieve Cory also had a lively phrase, "If this content doesn't present visually, call it radio." That's right on target! The media should match the need. This
notion, along with an integrated delivery approach, can provide "harmony" for
the viewers.

The National Association of Educational Broadcasting is doing a review and
analysis of all the open-learning systems activities that have taken place thus far
in the United States. It's just starting and Dr. Jim Fellows of NAEB is the project
director. I hope that there will be some link resulting from this meeting with his
effort, and you all will provide individual inputs to this endeavor. Those of you
who are interested in combining cable with the open-learning activities may wish
to get in touch with Jim and see that your input is shared in that study.

There's been considerable discussion about new institutions. We're maybe responding to a syndrome conditioned by our technological society. It's a replacement syndrome which says, "Here's the problem. Put in a new part." Whatever this informal institution does—and again I stress informal—I hope that it will combine a harmonious mixture of the old with the exciting new, as contrasted to setting up something completely new.

I hope that we'll all strive to seek responsible solutions which combine continuing education and cable in whatever ways that best maximize both the media and man. And I think I'd reverse the order and say, "Maximize mankind's potentials and the media."

Gerald S. Lesser

I am a great believer in success, especially visible success. Without doing a promotional piece for "Sesame Street," I do think that simply being able to point to one program with serious educational purposes that has attracted a large audience of young kids really has expedited a lot of things that have followed. Even one small successful model of a collaboration between cable operators and producers, or maybe between local businessmen and educators, might provide a momentum that doesn't exist at the moment. I don't know of one successful instance to date, and I don't know where that one visible success is going to come from, but there have been a number of ideas exchanged during this meeting that might provide the impetus for one. We will come at least closer to extended collaboration between cable operators and educators when we can say, "Look, we've done it, it can happen this way." You need to find a genius and then turn him loose. But you must find some way of not creating constraints and impositions that wreck that genius. We may have more geniuses than we know, but they are being buried under constraints that prevent them from operating.

Michael McCrudden

A lot more could be done right now than any one single entity is capable of doing. The cable operator alone is not capable of doing the best job possible; but as a cable operator, American Television and Communications would welcome advice, encouragement and suggestions as to what projects we should undertake and how to start tomorrow morning.

The one other thing we should all keep in mind as we think of these next steps is that while we have purposely talked about cable as it exists today, we should also start talking about two-way cable. It would be wrong to leave the conference with the idea that cable is a one-way delivery system, because whether or not the feedback is slow or fast, a feedback mechanism is going to be available in the immediate future. There exists in my mind a great potential, and perhaps an entirely different kind of potential, for two-way cable that we don't know anything about today. In a few years there are going to be substantial numbers of people who could be reached if we can find the money, the technology, and the right kind of teaching and learning techniques to use two-way cable.

Two-way cable will allow the educator to have some feel for what is going on in the world of the learner, and, secondly, it will allow that learner to be participating with the educator or with other learners. To a significant extent it will provide the potential for direct involvement by a mass of viewers. As we develop pilot projects, we must think of ways that we can take advantage of the new technology. It is not very far down the road, and it may be the real breakthrough for cable and continuing education.

Forrest Chisman

I personally think public access is the most exciting development in the video world today, but the idea of "participatory television" is not what we are concerned with here. The one link-up I see with education is that this allows some people to get a better idea of what television is about generally and to overcome some kinds of alienation. The better general understanding of television in the academic community may be important in moving ahead.

I think there have been two spectres at this banquet. One spectre has been the lack of leadership in this field. That is terribly important, especially from the funder's point of view. People come in all the time with good ideas which all look the same. You figure that you don't have very much money; and if the field itself is not setting priorities for you, and it is not central to your concern, you don't really want to set priorities yourself. As a result, funds are not made available as often as they might be otherwise.

The other spectre is the quality of the software. It is fine to say "Let a thousand flowers bloom," and we should make use of what we have now. But most people I know and respect in the field don't feel that most of the existing software is very good. Software would be one area in which to develop leadership. The CTW model is appropriate here, because good software is what is really going to involve people, not only in the educational world, but elsewhere, and at all levels. If you can show them something really big and really pretty, it's going to make them feel that this is a serious, important field to which they should pay attention. Now I know that that's a crude way to look at it, but that is my feeling about how to develop leaders in this field. They must come in with beautiful things in their briefcases and put them on the desk. One should not be overly concerned about thinking big in this field, because that is what is mainly needed now. I think "a great leap forward" wouldn't be a bad idea at the present time.

Shafeek Nader

Here is a quotation from a brochure that I have on Bilingual Children's Television: "Television audiences are the largest ever known in the history of communications, influencing more powerfully than any previous systems available to society. Furthermore, there is no question about whether it teaches, but rather a question of what it teaches, intentionally or unintentionally." I think there is a message here: Teaching and learning are going on in programming. Educational forces, by whatever means, must go to the area where things are happening and help to shape and influence them. For example, there should be several task groups or full-time operational advising groups to consult with commercial video production operations on content.

Another over-riding issue to grapple with is an all-inclusive definition of what constitutes continuous education and whether or not there is a symbolic, thought-triggering difference between continuing education and continuing learning. I would recommend that the Aspen Program on Communications and Society undertake the responsibility to keep a continuous formulation of an all-inclusive definition underway and to modify it from time to time.

Financing is a third area. We are trying really to break out of an information vacuum as far as the average person is concerned and to provide more relevant and necessary information to anyone who wants it. It isn't impossible to think along the lines of a trust fund that would help to finance and develop learning programs. It isn't impossible to ride on the back of social security mechanisms at a fraction of a percentage that could be allocated into a learning trust fund. Presently all the social security goes into the general fund.

There are some operations that could serve as models for the use of an educational channel, though not many. Linn-Benton is one; Oregon State University at Corvallis is another. But there is still a need for many other models for the use of education channels. How can a variety of educational organizations in a specific service area come together to make decisions about the use of time on a particular channel or to explore together how they might want to run some common programs? If on 10 o'clock on Tuesday morning the high school, the community college and the university all want to use that channel, who arbitrates? There's a real need to create a mechanism to do this. In addition, several models drawn from practical experiences should be published so that those communities that have no experience can at least have a point of departure, can take this model and say, "OK, let's start building a tradition."

Finally, I think there is a sleeper in the use of cable communications and that is the use of radio signals, orginated on the cable net or re-transmitted from over the air. Radio is something that has been overlooked by a majority of telecommunications interests; and it ought to be re-examined. It has a place in the mosaic of media. And if it put the cables to work, it might improve subscriptions.

Sig Mickelson

I would like to re-emphasize the point that you should not automatically discard the idea of making use of existing materials. Two of the best shows in the history of television were "Victory at Sea," which was made up entirely out of stock footage, and "Twentieth Century," which was also made out of stock footage until the later stages, when they started producing new and original materials.

I would also like to point out that software is the second step down the line. The first step must be an analysis of the needs and requirements of society matched against the unique characteristics and capabilities of electronic technologies for meeting those requirements. On so many occasions people have seen electronic communications technology and they've said, without thinking, "let's use it." When I was at CBS, for example, I had quite a shocking call from an officer on the staff of the Committee for Economic Development. He said, "We think the CED should have a television program. Won't you have lunch with me one of these days so we can talk about what that television program ought to be." It seems to me important to say that the way to use this new technology is to determine how it can best be used, and then use it only for those purposes.

David G. Hill

At this conference, I am neither fish nor fowl. I'm not an educator nor am I a representative of the communications media. Nevertheless, I have found my frustrations shared with everyone in this room. I had expected to find advanced communications between the media people and the educators. This was obviously not an accurate assessment. The most important information I will take away from this conference is the knowledge of where to go to find what is available in both areas.

I have heard many people here say, "this is my responsibility, and that responsibility is yours." No one indicated how it can all be put together to become a viable, functioning, widely used program. I tend to be more action-oriented. Therefore, I intend to try to generate movement in this area in the state of Ohio. I am extremely turned on by the possibility of technology—and I use that word rather than cable—as it relates to education in a non-traditional sense. This concept is very personal to my way of thinking, since it relates to a segment of the populace in Ohio with whom I greatly identify. It relates to people who haven't had the opportunity of pursuing higher education and those people who have been turned off by a system which is so entrenched with concepts of how one is educated.

I intend to see that the areas dealt with in this conference are given a full hearing. Recommendations coming from this committee will be sent to our governor and legislators. It is a perfect time to try to change some of the traditonal concepts in higher education as they operate in the state of Ohio.

As you all know, higher education is a give and take situation. I'm the only minority regent on our board, and until three months ago, we never had a woman on the board. When first appointed, I discovered the average age of the board was about 62, and immediately there developed a communications barrier. As I got to know my fellow regents better, I discovered each seemed to have a vested interest in certain constituencies—banking institutions, farmers, big business, etc. There was no one representing people who had never had the opportunity of getting into the system. At this point I promised myself, if I did nothing else as a regent, I had to try to bring in the people who have been denied access to the educational system. It's not a martyr role. Once you've been given an opportunity of doing something like this you have no choice. This conference has given me new ideas on how to accomplish some of my goals, and I'm committed to using some of the concepts as tools to change higher education in Ohio.

Genevieve Cory

For me, this conference has been an incomparable and valuable experience, but I have one very deep concern. The verbal and written emphasis here has been on continuing education with groups that you understand, groups that are very nearly like you, groups that respond to traditional educational modes, and, importantly, groups that return observable and tangible results to you that reward your efforts and sustain you.

I'd like to put in a plea that you give the educational problems of the poor a higher priority. By this I mean that subset of people at the lower one-third of the economic scale. These people are the ones who have generally rejected institutionalized education. They are the people who need a kind of education in the area of competency for day-to-day living that has not been readily available. I have a deep hunch that each individual in this category has to have a certain minimal level of personal competency before much acquisition of formal and traditional content can take place.

I have a deep concern about the urgency of this because there are converging social forces that I fear greatly. Let's look at these social forces: There is the population explosion; there is increasing pollution; there are housing and food shortages; and there is crime. All these fears are now being coupled with the inexorable findings of genetics and the knowledge gleaned from child development that points to irreversible damage from inadequate early nourishment. It all adds up to intensifying the general attitude of, "Who needs you?" We don't give a damn. Compassion is running out.

The competence gap in our society is widening not narrowing. Societal changes are coming so fast that each individual has to absorb and process an increasing number of bits of information even to stay afloat. Formerly competent people are sinking; more and more human beings are being spun off from the edges of competency into the mass of those who can't cope. I would just like to leave the thought that you should address yourselves to these humanistic needs. You simply can't leave out this group of people.

Cyril Houle

I'm a professor full time, a group which seems to be getting its lumps this morning. I am also, as it happens, a professor of adult and continuing education and what I preach to other people I feel should apply to me. I came here to learn and I've learned a lot.

In learning, of course, one always builds upon past knowledge. Two comments of Andre Malraux in his *Museum Without Walls* have struck me as being particularly appropriate to this discussion. One of his comments is that every new invention begins by being constricted by previous inventions and tries to imitate them. If you went to the Aspen Crystal Palace last night, for example, you saw the old automobiles which looked like buggies. In the early days, such cars even had sockets for buggy whips. The development of the automobile has grown as it has moved away from the idea of imitating the buggy. And of course, the film freed itself of being a photographed stage play only when D. W. Griffith moved in for close-ups and began to use the film as a medium on its own. I have the very strong sense that cable television is still in the stage of imitating certain previous inventions. It will naturally move, but it will take time and it will take the genius of people like D. W. Griffith, to move away from present prototypes.

I was reminded of another point of Malraux's by Douglass Cater's statement that cable television is retail rather than wholesale. Malraux's point in *Museum Without Walls* is essentially that good photographic reproduction of pictures made possible not merely more people having more pictures on their walls, but a qualitative difference as well. Formerly to study art you would have to travel to all the castles in Europe, and you would forget one painting as you saw another. When adequate color photographic reproductions became available, you could compare paintings and thereby discover kinds of relationships which were never previously possible. As cable television develops, particularly along the line of diversity—having many different channels and many different opportunities and possibilities for comparision—it is going to create new combinations of aesthetic and educational experience which will make qualitative differences we do not yet comprehend.

W. Bowman Cutter

As we plan for the use of cable, I hope that we don't take too seriously the gloom about cable that has generally been in all of our messages. We must plan for the systems that are emerging, because they do offer two things: a considerable capacity for variety, and a progressive capacity to adapt to individual needs. These are two of the things that should interest people who are experts in continuing education. I think the cable systems that are emerging in our larger cities and communities throughout the country are going to be quite sophisticated. They don't deserve the gloom.

We spoke a great deal also about the use of mixed media. One of my disappointments is that we haven't gotten specific enough instructions from the educators here about "What do you want to do?" Not necessarily on cable but on almost anything. I'd like to see the Aspen Institute sponsor the development of a set of scenarios for the use of specific types or mixes of media—a set of thought experiments. For example, how would you do a career counseling and vocational program of the type that Jim Gibbons has been suggesting?

Beyond that, I have some skepticism about the immediate use of existing materials. I hope it's done; I know it's going to get done. My skepticism relates to two points, which we've tried to deal with. The first is simply the quality of the software available, and the second has to do with the definition of our ends. If we go about suffused with good intentions and a sense of social need and start throwing films on cable systems, I'm not sure that the end result is going to be a happy one. "Victory at Sea," which, as Sig Mickelson mentioned, was a marvelous program, took an awful lot of planning, an awful lot of work.

Like Jerry Lesser, I'd like to see a success for cable education. Find the entrepreneurs and the geniuses and then leave them alone. I think that leaving them alone is more important than the genius part of that sentence. If you find good people and leave them alone, they generally do very good things. And then, finally, I'm more convinced than I was in the earlier discussions that there is a definite need for some form of national institution that deals with the assessment and distribution of software.

Amos Hostetter

Let me try to organize what I have heard here in terms of various levels of abstraction of the problem. The problem at the first level of abstraction is: What can society do to improve the life-long process of education, to determine what education really should be and what function it should perform. Unfortunately, this question is a long way from where I am on a day-to-day basis; and I find it hard to identify what tangible help I can offer in dealing with this problem.

The bridge by which we get to the next level of abstraction seems to me to be Tom James' statement of the "The Iron Law of Education," which basically is that costs in education are going up faster than productivity and that the amount of our total output committed to education is therefore on a collision course with total output itself. Based on this proposition, the question becomes, "What are the cost-effective uses of the new technologies in education?" This basic question has occupied a good deal of our conversation. In the process, the cable people here have been exposed, in my case for the first time, to a set of sub-problems and obstacles which apparently the educators have recognized for some time. These relate to the educational establishment's resistance to change, the massive inertia of institutions and attitude sets, in particular the accreditation system which has been built. Fundamentally, it appears we have a rather frozen system of allocating any quantity of dollars within education.

I came here with what I thought was a very neat construct for talking about cable and education. It is Shumpeter's concept of creative displacement as a way of describing the way we shift productivity curves and expand real output. According to that theory, the way real growth is accomplished is not by additions, but by productive substitution. We replace buggies with automobiles, and as applied here, we should be talking about replacing bricks, mortar and talking heads with the new audio-visual technologies. In this framework we can talk about re-allocations of resources presently committed to education and are not forced to propose massive additions of funding. Independent of how desirable such additions might be, it seems to me to be highly impractical to rest our hopes on such a solution. We must deal with an essentially fixed "nut."

The comments that were the most sobering to me here, that in effect shattered my neat little model, were the ones that highlighted the terrific obstacle we're up against in attempting to make these re-allocations within the educational system. The institutions of education seem intolerably rigid, establishing self-reinforcing priorities and allocations around the almighty "full-time equivalency." It now seems to me that before there can be any hope of new technologies making an impact on education, we've got to free up the mechanisms of allocating funds within the educational system. If, as some here have said, this is so inimical to the present institutions of education as to be impossible, then we should focus on fostering new, less frozen, institutions now developing in the government, community colleges and private educational sectors.

Thus, the problem at the next level of abstraction is "What can we do to relax and break down the set patterns of the institutions and cartels in education?" Even at this level, I find it hard to see what I can contribute as a result of our discussions. Although I do think I understand the problem better for having been here, I believe that this problem must really be solved by the educators. It would clearly be helpful to the educators' efforts here to have some demonstrable examples of cost-effective applications of the new technologies in education, but here, too, I find it hard to identify a constructive role for myself. Audio/video is only one component of the new technologies, and cable is only one delivery mode for audio/video. Thus cable is only a small sub-subset of the new technologies.

The task of creating demonstrably effective video applications in education is really a joint task of the educators and video production and creative types. But to be honest, cable people, at least those here, do not represent the producers, the talent, the creators of product. Television production skills are employed today primarily in the broadcast system; they're not in the cable business. In this area we must look to the few successes educational television has produced in its 20-year struggle, and CTW is one outstanding model. It seems to me that only after we get a good sense of useful video applications to education, can we begin to talk about cable as an aid in those applications.

Given my improved understanding of this hierarchy, I reiterate my feeling that there is little I can do today to help solve these problems. The Sam Goulds must deal with redefining the role and mode of education in society. The Dave Hills must deal with the creation of an allocation system which is less dependent on bricks and more dependent on new technologies. The Joan Cooneys must deal with developing constructive video applicable in education.

In wrapping up, I wish you all well, because it's absolutely essential that these problems be solved. Lest this appear to be a cop-out, let me reiterate a consistent theme of the cable operators here. We are an available and eager conduit for any responsible applications of broadband technology in education. Just tell us when and what we can do to help. I am very much oriented toward the school of "one small step for man," but I am profoundly frustrated after our session with how little we as cable people can do to advance the ball on our own initiative.

Frank Dobyns

There are ways in which we can learn very quickly about the future, and I think that one of them hinges on this notion of the entrepreneur. We ought to get cracking with some of these entrepreneurs out there to get some projects started in which you spot a need, get it very clearly in mind, and then develop a response. In this instance, I'm thinking of the software. Produce it, measure its effectiveness and make it available. I say you'll learn a lot. I say you'll be able to find the geniuses, because they're out there. In fact, I claim that if you were to do a few very specific pilot projects, you would learn enough about how to put together the kind of team so that you'd be able to replicate them.

Frank Lloyd Wright had the right idea when he would say to people, "Look, tell me what it is you want to do in that building. Then I'll help you design the building and say, "Now get in." That has been much of the problem with technology. Technology ought to be society's idea on how you solve problems more effectively. Cable is a good example. There was a problem: Some people couldn't get television transmission. Well, then give them a cable system. The technology was trying to solve a problem. That is where we should be looking.

James Miller

Of the many things I could say, I'm going to concentrate on one thing: For another session we should try to develop a unified conceptual system. Nothing elicits agreement among people of disparate points of view more effectively than trying to agree on a unitary conceptual approach. Among other things, we need to have a taxonomy of the types of human systems and media that we're concerned with.

We must first identify the living systems that are involved. The most important one is the individual learner, if we're talking about education; the individual user if we're talking about cable TV. Then there are groups like the family or the classroom, and there are organizations like school systems, universities and cities made up of these lower levels; and there are societies, like the United States, with national policy concerns. Someday, also, I hope we look at the international level. Now, given these levels, I think that we still should emphasize primarily the creation of the appropriate learning environment around the individual learner and how the higher levels can be restructured.

To do this conceptually, we need, first of all, to define the boundary of the particular system we're talking about at a given moment. We've been shifting without noticing it from one of these levels to another in our discussions here, without declaring what specific concrete system we are dealing with and without describing it explicitly. I would hope we would in future discussions impose on ourselves certain constraints in discussion that would enable us during a given session to deal with a concrete town or city. We could perhaps even picture it graphically, marking or diagramming it in a way that would facilitate a group analysis of it.

Once we have decided on the boundaries of the particular level of system we want, then we should identify the sub-systems that make up a community, and find out how we can use media in each of these systems—from the transducers that bring the information in, like the microphone and the camera, through the channels that convey it, to the output machine with which the human being who is doing the learning interacts.

At the next meeting like this, I suggest three things:

1. developing a conceptual system or alternative conceptual systems;
2. either discussing only one of the media (*e.g.,* video or audio) and considering all the alternatives for using it, or discussing all the various possible trade-offs among the full set of electronic information processing media for a given single use;
3. choosing a specific system—a city, a society or perhaps a university—and analyzing in some detail what cable TV can do for it.

Charlotte Jones

One of the things that has struck me about this conference is that I get the sense that we all come with a certain vested interest, constituency, focus of attention and priorities. But it is not necessarily true that our various interests are mutually exclusive of one another, although I frequently get the feeling that some of us feel that they are. For example, one of you said that the imprimatur of excellence that would come to a new model which was designed and funded well would make everyone sit up and take notice. I agree, but at the same time I don't think that concept is mutually exclusive with finding existing materials and using them.

I don't know much about the money problems that have been raised, but in my limited exposure, one of the difficulties seems to be in not sharing the expertise of faculties among the campuses. If materials were developed that could be shared, it seems to me it would be a very small next step to bring that same material out into the community from the campuses.

I was very moved by Genevieve's eloquent statement about human values. And that, too, is not a mutually exclusive comment to everything else that we are doing. It is terribly important for us to remind ourselves at all times that everything we do must always be cognizant of those human values and be directed toward them. That kind of thing is something that cable can and should do—drug abuse information, welfare rights information, tenant's rights information, housing information, employment information and so on. It is something that we absolutely should feel obligated to get involved in.

Jay Raeben

My comment is directed toward future conferences and goes to what may have been an assumption underlying this conference. Those concerned with continuing education are, in fact, not likely to deal directly with cable systems except for local programs. Many educators' relationships with cable will be through companies such as our own. There are many large companies in what can loosely be termed the information business, and many of these have a great interest in cable and cassettes. They have a lot of sophistication, a lot of interesting ideas, and some ability to take risks. They are going to play an important role in the development of uses of cable in continuing education and ought to be represented more prominently in future meetings that you hold. Lest anyone think that this would give the conference too commercial a cast, I'd like to give you my belief that both humanistic values, on the one hand, and territoriality, on the other, are qualities that are inherent in individuals and not in their vocations.

Barry Zorthian

In these meetings, a re-occurring theme seemed to emerge which is fairly obvious, I guess. There is a great and growing desire for knowledge—I refuse to be bound by the word "education." At the same time, there is a growing technical capacity to serve that need. Cable is one such communication system which will be very important and very significant for the future.

I recognize some of the comments about gloom from other participants may be directed toward me. I assure you I am not gloomy about cable or I wouldn't be in the business. But I do see a need to remove some euphoria about it and to be realistic. Cable is going to give our society some enormous capacity, as are these other media—video cassettes, some of the uses of laser, a great many other things that are still in the laboratory stage. The challenge is what we do with these essentially neutral physical means, and that challenge is what we've been talking about here. We have barely scratched the surface, it's such a broad challenge. I leave this meeting with some feeling that educators have not been aggressive enough about these opportunities, at least as a general group. I deduce this from your words, not my own calculation. I gather you yourselves feel you didn't do well enough with educational television, with certain exceptions, over the past 20 years.

That to me is both a disappointment and an opportunity. I came here with a cable-system operator's hat but also with an information company's hat, and I expect to go back to my company and say I think there is an opening here. If we consciously go about exploiting it, the opening may be greater than we think. I'm not sure the educators institutionally are going to be able to meet the demand; and if our company can tap some of the talent and expertise in the educational system and combine it with our readiness to market and our venture capital, we can help meet this desire for information on a profitable basis. We can come up with new forms, new mixes.

I don't know that education with a capital E has to be separated from private enterprise. The great communications conglomerates that are growing in this country are going to get into the business of education, or, if you will, of providing information. Maybe this is an area that hasn't been probed enough. Maybe there is a great deal of potential in putting your talents together with business firms to meet this enormous demand. There is nothing wrong with private business, with venture capital, getting into this area and meeting some of these challenges. It's an area that ought to be probed more. It's certainly one that I would recommend for my company through whatever means we have. I would urge that a four-way combination of the cable system owner, the hardware owner, the private businessman investor, and the educator develop these possibilities with great benefit to society as a whole.

Jack McBride

My crystal ball shows that for the next several years, American education and the public television industry will be getting increasingly involved in continuing education, producing a considerably greater quantity of courseware and programming. It shows the endeavors to be mixed in terms of success—some highly successful, some moderately, some failures. It shows also that the program courseware won't be produced exclusively or explicitly for cable or for broadcast. Instead, it will be produced and used interchangeably over broadcast, over cable and on video cassettes, in order to try to get maximum value from the materials. It shows also that the quality of product is going to be even more of a problem over the next several years for all the reasons that have been stated earlier. Finally, it shows that there really are going to be relatively few places where quality materials are going to be produced. Therefore, it is going to be extremely important to husband the resources as much as possible and make sure that those few producers of quality educational products talk to one another and don't dissipate their energy and resources re-inventing the wheel.

I'll close with a plea. Somewhere, somehow, sometime, somebody had better start devoting some attention to the problem of how to get the viewer, the student, the one out there who needs all this information and education, motivated to watch all of this programming we plan to send down the line. And not only motivated to turn on the set the first time, but motivated to keep coming back, time and time again, to learn what really needs to be learned. Very little attention has been given to this problem. Somebody better start, because we can spend untold amounts of money, time, energy and talent producing high quality materials that might otherwise just go for naught.

Frank Norwood

I hear in our conversations a dichotomy between whether we ought to approach continuing education by creating a new Childrens Television Workshop, or whether we should start with whatever existing materials we have. The answer is probably "yes" in both cases. They are not mutually exclusive. I'm a great admirer of Joan Cooney and the CTW, but I think that it is also important that we begin where we are. There are some materials that are not as good as we will someday have. We can't wait for the creation of those materials.

We should look toward a pilot sometime in the future, but we should also look now toward experiments. CTW didn't begin by cloistering itself and then suddenly having one program. It went out and tested the market. We are now in that position. We should begin immediately, using the best of existing materials and looking at what we do as a series of experiments. Too often, we get into pilots and if the pilot doesn't work, then we think we've done the wrong thing. Scientists know that an experiment is something you learn from. We may learn how insufficient the kinds of software we now have are, so that we can design software that is adequate.

Although we are looking toward establishing new institutions, we must depend very heavily on the institutions that already exist. For example, a question was raised about whether new emerging institutions ought to have a separate accrediting agency. In my judgment, that would be a disaster. What we do has got to be judged by standards that apply to all. If we make up new rules, anything we do will be dismissed, regardless of how stringent our rules might be. Furthermore, we've got to take advantage of the fact that there are new forces in the field that are going to help us develop new programming. We should not create a continuing learning workshop that will go off by itself and invent new software. We should tap what's happening in emerging institutions—what Jessie Hartline is doing in New Jersey, what Jack McBride is doing in Nebraska, what other institutions are going to be doing, Dave Hill's interest in the possibility that Ohio may be able to do some things in this area.

The number of dollars that are available from the public till may be shrinking, but we are now talking about some people who are motivated to spend their own discretionary funds. That may represent entirely new sources of dollars that do not require cutbacks somewhere else. With all these new forces emerging, a wise investment of our time and whatever resources we can bring together would be working to harness these forces, rather than gong out and attempting to create another new set of forces independent of what is presently going on.

Armand Hunter

Since a seminar of this type is a continuing education and a learning experience, let me recommend it to you, even though you may have gone through the process with very high levels of frustration and discomfiture at times. We probably should not expect closure in any form at a seminar of this nature, because we have too many people of very different backgrounds, different experiences and different interests. We have had a constant shifting of ideas, of problems, of questions; and this constant shift, coupled with the variety of individuals, simply produces a kind of broad-based variety of concerns and questions that practically forbids any kind of wrap-up.

One of the questions that we have wrestled with here is the infinite number of parts and the complexity of the problems. All of us recognize the variety of the parts of the issues, and yet we have a compulsion to try to bring these into some kind of a system, into a relationship that will add up to some whole greater than the sum of the parts. Many of the comments that Jim Miller made about a conceptual design that could move in this direction are excellent ones.

One of the things that is always a problem is the matter of definition of terms. When we talk about continuing education, this means many things to many people. There are two elements of the term that should be separated. When we talk about continuing education and continuing learning, or life-long education and life-long learning, we tend to use them in much the same sense, and that's confusion of the terms. I think semantically they each mean something different. Life-long learning or continuing learning is a function of the individual, and that is infinite. That is something which I don't believe can be systematized or put into a package. But if you are talking about life-long education or continuing education, you are talking about the order and design, the structuring and the distribution of knowledge. This I think can be systematized. And it is at this point that the institutions concerned with education can perhaps come together to develop a design for the systematic and organized provision of resources for the vast, unsystematic and unorganized need for life-long learning.

The struggle to arrive at a point of singleness of some conceptual design or purpose bothers me a little bit. The situation is somewhat like the professor who had always wanted to play the cello. One year his wife bought him a cello for Christmas, whereupon he seized his new cello, retired into his study and proceeded to play all morning, all afternoon and all evening. The problem was, he was playing just one note. His wife stood this as long as she could and then went into the study and said, "Dear I'm so happy that you are enjoying your Christmas present, but I notice that when other people play their cellos, they run their fingers up and down the strings and produce different notes." He looked at her for a moment and said, "Others are looking for the note. I have found it."

We're looking for a note. I know we haven't found it, but I sometimes feel that perhaps we'd better run our fingers up and down the strings. In that respect, we may be able to make more music. With the other procedure, we may end up with just sheer noise.

The Next Steps:
A Summary of Conference Proposals

6

The first day of the Aspen Workshop conference was devoted to discussions of the current states of continuing education and cable television. The second day consisted of reports on on-going projects using television (primarily broadcast) for extramural education. The participants also considered the role which cable could play as a new delivery system for continuing education. Then, on the third day of the workshop, the participants split into two groups to discuss what new initiatives were needed to make effective use of cable. One group explored actions which could be taken locally; the other was concerned with national initiatives. The recommendations produced by these two discussion groups, and the discussions which led to them, are summarized below.

Local Initiatives

The successful uses of cable for continuing education are modest and few in number, nor is there much evidence of concrete planning at present. However, there is considerable and growing interest in many communities in the educational potential of cable. The following three proposals were designed by the discussion group to encourage the channeling of this community interest into planning for specific uses of the cable, both in communities with existing systems and in communities in which systems are to be built:

1. Proposal: That a practical guide to the use of cable for education, and the educational access channel in particular, be produced.

As cable becomes established in a community, the focus of interest will shift from the issues of franchising to questions about the utilization of cable channels. For such communities, there is now a clear need for specific information on how educators can work with cable operators. Bowman Cutter reported that the Cable Television Information Center has already received approximately 500 requests for help of this kind. He pointed out that although the FCC requires that a channel be reserved for "educational access," the commission has little guidance as to its use and users.

A practical guide for local educational authorities and cable operators is clearly needed. These are the people who will determine the success or failure of the channels. The discussion group also agreed that the guide should deal not only with continuing education but with the whole broad range of uses of the educational-access channel.

Bowman Cutter stated that the Cable Television Information Center would undertake the responsibility for producing a guide to the educational-access channel. Such a guide might suggest "a series of scenarios for the use of that channel" and would describe possible means of cooperation between the educational officials who have been given the authority to use the channel and the operators who retain ultimate administrative responsibility for it. In conclusion, it was noted that the FCC rules stipulate that the experience of the access channels will be reviewed after five years, at which time the channels may be eliminated or expanded on the basis of that review. The group therefore agreed that encouraging successful uses of the educational-access channel is a matter of some urgency if its continued existence is to be assured.

2. Proposal: That a commitment be made by the largest multiple system cable operators to identify one or more target cable systems that would cooperate with local educational institutions in offering continuing education courses via cable. Educators in these communities would work with the national ETV libraries to explore the suitability of existing courseware for local use. An effort would also be made to survey and catalog existing materials in these libraries and other commercial sources.

The question of the usefulness of existing instructional materials for cable-cast continuing education was debated at length by the workshop as a whole and by the discussion group participants. Some participants felt strongly that existing course materials were of poor quality and were largely responsible for the disappointing record of instructional television to date. Frank Norwood pointed out that for the most part "instructional television has been merely televised instruction" and that it would be a mistake for education via cable to follow this tradition. While agreeing that much—if not most—of what has been produced is ineffective, other participants felt that some excellent materials did exist. The problem, they felt, was that there is no convenient mechanism for finding and utilizing these materials. As a result, successes remain isolated, with little influence beyond their immediate sphere.

The group agreed that the attractiveness of the above proposal was that it could be carried out rapidly and without the need of substantial outside funding. Such an experiment would encourage the development of working relationships between operators and educators, would focus attention on the operational problems of such relationships, and could provide immediate educational bene-fits to cable subscribers. And if these experiments succeeded, they could then become the basis for proposing an adequately funded national effort to review and catalog the usefulness of existing course materials for continuing education.

3. *Proposal: That a high-visibility pilot project be conducted to test the use-fulness of cable for continuing education. The project would be carried out in a community with a sizable cable system and several educational institu-tions already offering continuing education. The project would survey ex-pressed interest in further education, develop and offer courses in response to those interests, and measure the student responses to the courses and their effectiveness.*

This project represents a longer range, more ambitious undertaking than that envisioned in the previous proposal. It would be a carefully conceived research project, requiring outside funding and lasting over a period of several years. The project would be carried out in a reasonably representative city with an operating cable system and one or more institutions (public, private or proprietary) willing to offer a range of credit and non-credit courses over cable. The purposes of the project would be

- To develop a better survey system to determine interest in various educa-tional offerings;
- To determine actual participation in televised courses as compared with ex-pressed interest;
- To develop a model for collaboration between educational institutions and commercial cable operators;
- To develop course materials specifically designed for home-based continuing education via cable;
- To attract public attention to the potential of television-supported education.

Some existing courses might be used in the early stages of the project, but the goal of the project would be the offering of new courses produced specifically in response to community needs. The suggested program areas on which such a project might concentrate included vocational and career guidance, high school or college-level academic courses, and "game" programs with an educational component for parents and children.

National Initiatives

The second group of conference participants spent a morning considering development of cablecast continuing education and the initiatives and strategies that were needed on a national level for the success of such programs. There was a clear consensus that efficient development of continuing education on cable depends upon the creation of a national mechanism for sharing information and instructional materials for post-secondary education. Perhaps the most dramatic statement of this need came from Amos Hostetter, who offered the proposition that in the absence of "major [federal] commitment, educational applications of the 'new technologies' will be developed largely outside of existing educational institutions and in approximately inverse order of humanistically defined need." Although this statement was not endorsed by all of the participants in the discussion, there was general agreement that national intiatives were needed to promote cooperative efforts and to prevent the proliferation of mediocrity.

The discussion group expressed caution about any national strategy that would have the effect of putting the cart of technology before the horse of education. It is still not certain how large a role cable will play compared to cassette or to other possible delivery systems for education. Therefore, alternative systems must be explored fully and imaginatively, without allowing bias toward a particular technology to condition the choices made. The group agreed that the most serious barriers to increasing access to continuing education are not technological but the lack of information and institutional arrangements to support it.

Specifically, the major "national" needs of continuing education today were seen by the discussion group as the following:

- The training of those involved in continuing education for the effective use of new technologies. This is of highest priority. Unless educators understand the proper uses of technology, their resistance to it will be continually crippling;
- The development of various components of courseware for a variety of educational objectives;
- A better dissemination of information and existing materials;
- The identification of various financial mechanisms for the support of continuing education;
- A systematization of the processes of exploration and implementation.

In arriving at its recommendations, the discussion group agreed on two principles which should underlie any national initiatives and strategy: First, the development of profit and non-profit enterprises should be encouraged simultaneously; and second, the initial emphasis in the development of continuing education via cable should be on the paying audience, with the possible use of government subsidy to extend that audience.

Based on these two principles, the following recommendations were offered to and endorsed by the conference participants:

1. Proposal: That a joint market-research study be co-sponsored by education and the cable industry to derive information about the potential audience for televised continuing education.

A great deal remains to be learned about the nature and interests of those who are now being referred to as "non-traditional students." The work of Moses and Johnstone and Rivera* revealed the enormous numbers of students not engaged in full-time study; the research of the Commission on Non-Traditional† Study indicated that many more would pursue further education if it were available to them. In order to create a system which is responsive to these interests, specific answers are needed for such questions as: What are the educational priorities of potential learners? Are they interested in taking courses via television? How much are they willing to pay? How important is credit? How greatly will the answers to these questions vary from community to community?

Several participants reported undertaking surveys of this kind as part of their projects: Dean Hartline described a survey being undertaken for the Open University in New Jersey, and Jack McBride stated that S-U-N had decided on the first courses it would produce on the basis of a survey in Nebraska. However, the survey proposed by the discussion group as a whole would be oriented toward the interests of current and potential cable subscribers and whether they and their interests differ markedly from the general population. Barry Zorthian pointed out that with approximately 20 million homes to be wired for cable in the next decade, the results of such a survey could influence which cities and towns should be wired. He noted that although there are, of course, many other factors that go into making such decisions, the educational market should be one of the elements being considered. Other cable operators in the group expressed doubt whether interest in educational programming would be great enough to affect cable operators' decisions about placement, but all agreed that the only way of resolving this question would be to carry out the survey.

2. Proposal: That a major study of the means for financing expanded access to continuing education be carried out.

Much of continuing education in this country—including university extension services—has traditionally operated on the basis of paying its own way. Pay-cable, with its ability to limit access to those who pay for it, permits the extension of this concept to televised instruction. The "Edu-Cable" plan described in Part II even envisions a profit-making scheme for the delivery of education via pay-cable. While such a scheme may prove financially viable, it might do little to expand access to continuing education for those who most need it and are least able to afford it.

---

*See Chapter 1, p. 00.

†See Chapter 1, p. 00.

The question of whether the expansion of continuing education should be financed through public subsidy or should rely on direct consumer support was a question too large for the workshop to address adequately. Even if the use of technological delivery systems proves to be cost-effective, it seemed clear that to reach larger numbers of people with effective educational programs, educational institutions will have to meet increased expenditures. Where these funds should come from, and what priorities should be set in terms of expenditures for technology, are decisions which go well beyond the role of cable or any other specific delivery system. An issue of particular importance is establishing the federal role for subsidies in this area. Although there are problems with creating federal categorical programs at this time, using old money for new purposes has always proved to be very difficult to accomplish in education.

These questions are complex and require further attention. Therefore, the discussion group recommended that an agency such as the Aspen Program on Education for a Changing Society (APEX) undertake a broad study of the financing of continuing education.

3. Proposal: That a campaign be launched to educate educators to the potential uses of cable and other new technologies.

As several conference participants pointed out, educational technology has remained fixed on the periphery of the educational establishment. And until a greater understanding of its role is created among teachers and administrators, it is likely to remain there. To some degree, the academic respectability of telecommunications as an educational tool is linked to the value placed on extramural education and on the idea of creating an educational system more responsive to the interests and needs of its students. The work of the Carnegie Commission and the Commission on Non-Traditional Study have made substantial contributions to these movements and have helped to illuminate the place of technology within them.

What is needed now is an on-going effort to provide information to educators about the developing role of technology within education. In particular, the discussion group recommended that the American Council on Education—as the central coordinating body for higher education—provide a continuing forum to bring its member institutions and the various disciplinary associations face to face with the new technology and its entrepreneurs. Todd Furniss indicated that the A.C.E. does not have the resources to undertake large-scale research and information-collection without outside funding, but it does consider the dissemination of this kind of information to its members as part of its mandate. Furniss noted that this function is also served by the Joint Council on Educational Telecommunications—again, with limited resources.

4. Proposal: That a national system for the collection, assessment and distribution of instructional materials for post-secondary education be established. Such a system would not serve cable or continuing education exclusively, but it would aid both. The purpose of the system would be to promote the sharing of high quality materials and to avoid duplication of effort.

This proposal was the most vigorously debated of all those offered by the workshop discussion group. Many expressed fears that the scarcity of high quality materials and faculty resistance to materials produced elsewhere would frustrate the intent of such a system. Others argued that the recent American Open University experiments and the successful distribution of Miami-Dade's ecology course suggest that this situation may be changing. They agree that the existence of an effective national distribution system would encourage the production of high-quality materials by sharing the costs of production among multiple institutions.

It was the consensus of the conference participants that the creation of a new, autonomous agency was not necessary at this time. These functions could be served most efficiently by the expansion of one of the three existing national ITV libraries, which are already experienced in the distribution of materials at the elementary and secondary level. As in the case of the Great Plains National ITV Library, the system would almost certainly require start-up seed money— probably from federal funds—but it should be intended to work toward economic self-sufficiency as soon as possible.

5. *Proposal: That a continuing overview of progress in the use of cable and other communications technologies for continuing education be carried out by the Aspen Workshop on the Cable and Continuing Education.*

Many of the projects described at the conference were in their preliminary stages, and their success was still uncertain. The participants in the Aspen Workshop agreed that their conference represented a useful beginning in attempting to bring cable and continuing education together, but that the significance of the meeting would ultimately be determined by the concrete results which resulted from it. One of the most encouraging consequences of the conference was an agreement reached between Dean Hartline of Rutgers and Charlotte Schiff Jones of TelePrompTer Corporation to arrange for the cablecasting of courses from Rutgers Open University on one or more Teleprompter systems in New Jersey. Because of the potential significance of this project and the other conference proposals, participants asked that the Aspen Cable Workshop monitor progress on each of them and prepare a follow-up report within a year.

A Summary Statement

The Aspen Workshop conference concluded with a general agreement to the above proposals and an expression of guarded optimism about the opportunities provided by the confluence of the new communications technologies and the new interest in educational innovation. A cautionary theme which ran through the conference was that the identification of educational needs must come first and that cable and other technology must be considered as options in meeting those needs. Conference participants also agreed that a concerted effort will be required to exploit cable's potential for creating open access to continuing education. What is most needed now are one or more demonstrable successes which would serve as the impetus for further efforts.

PART II

The Southern California Regional
Consortium for Community College Television

In 1967 the Los Angeles ABC-affiliate station KABC-TV asked Pasadena City College to develop a college-level course to be broadcast over the station. It offered free use of production facilities and free broadcast time during low-demand early morning hours. The college responded affirmatively, and the result was a three-unit course in art history, consisting of broadcast lessons, supporting readings, telephone consultation between students and faculty, voluntary on-campus seminars, and required on-campus examinations. Nearly 1,800 students enrolled for credit the first semester.

Pasadena's success encouraged other community colleges in the region to join in a formal television consortium that now includes 26 institutions. It is guided by both a professional director (housed on the "neutral ground" of the Los Angeles County school system office) and a number of inter-institutional committees with responsibilities for (1) organization and legislation; (2) curriculum, innovation, instruction and evaluation; (3) promotion and publicity; and (4) production. By the end of the 1972-73 academic year, the consortium will have produced and offered the nine courses listed below, attracting enrollments now averaging over 5,000 students each term.

Each consortium member contributes $3,000 yearly, and this $78,000 budget covers general expenses plus the production of the one or two courses each year. All production to date has utilized the free facilities and personnel of commercial television stations; thus, the consortium now pays only for faculty time, graphics,

Term	Course	Enrollment
Fall 1970	Effective Living (health education)	380
	Psychology I	309
		689
Spring 1971	Law for the 70's (consumer law)	404
	Psychology I*	427
		831
Summer 1971	History of World Theatre	1,744
Fall 1971	Effective Living*	2,754
	History of Mexico	5,277
		8,031
Spring 1972	History of Art 1A*	3,549
	Law for the 70's*	3,407
		6,956
Fall 1972	Introduction to Astronomy	2,312
	History of Art 1A*	3,416
		5,728
Spring 1973	Physical Geography	–
	Consumer Education	–

tape and other materials, and similar non-studio costs. These costs for a three-unit course average about $20,000. In addition, the costs borne by the producing stations are estimated by the consortium director as ranging between $50,000 and $100,000 for the 45 half-hours of television included in each course.† Thus the production cost per hour is in the $3,000 to $5,000 range. The non-television incremental costs (primarily faculty salaries) for the consortium members are estimated at about $500 per campus for each course. Each campus can recover up to one-half of their consortium contribution and incremental costs from state funds; the rest comes from their general operating budgets.

Courses to be produced and offered are selected by an inter-institutional committee, which also selects the producing instructors after reviewing competing proposals. To date, courses have dealt with topics of broad interest primarily outside the list of courses required for the AA degree. This determination was made with an eye to appealing to a large audience while avoiding the threat to faculties that might be represented by broadcasting basic required courses.

Prior to the start of a course, a brochure is mailed out to potential students by each of the institutions which choose to participate. Those who decide to

---

*Repeated courses.

†For comparison, a nearby state university campus is now producing four similar courses in its own existing studios, using a good deal of student help, at a budgeted cost of only $25,000 per course.

take the course enroll at whichever of the sponsoring institutions they determine is most convenient to them (district boundaries are conveniently ignored by all concerned). Enrollment procedures are kept simple, requiring only the completion of a tear-out from the announcement brochure. Everyone who wishes credit is eligible, regardless of previous educational attainment. There is no charge to the student, and the only costs involved are for books or text materials. One of the participating institutions provides the text materials, and the student may order the materials by mail, utilizing another tear-out from the brochure.

· ·

TEAR HERE

APPLICATION FOR ENROLLMENT (check one or both):
___ HISTORY OF ART 1-A   ___ INTRODUCTION TO ASTRONOMY

Mr.
Mrs. _____
Miss   Last   First   Middle
Address_____
            Number   Street   City   Zip
Last enrolled at LA City or another college _____
                                    Name of College
Your name, when last enrolled, if different from above:
_____   Year _____
High School Attended _____ Year Grad. _____
College Units Completed:
___ None   ___ Sophomore – 60 or more
___ Freshman – ½ - 29½   ___ A. B. Degree
___ Sophomore – 30 - 59½ ___ A.B. Degree or higher
No. of units for which you are registering this semester:_____

I wish to take midterm and final
examinations at (name college): _____

Soc. Sec. No. _____ - _____ - _____
Birthdate _____
Birthplace _____
Telephone No. _____
Today's Date _____

Ethnic Background:
___ 1. American Indian
___ 2. Oriental
___ 3. Mexican-American
___ 4. Afro-American
___ 5. Other Non-white
___ 6. All other

Will you be enrolled for other courses while taking this TV course? If so, please indicate college:
_____
_____

Signed _____

INSTRUCTIONS: Print clearly.

Answer all items that apply to you. Mail to the Mailing Address of the college at which you wish to take your examinations.

Course programs are broadcast over a commercial station during low-audience early morning hours and over the local public broadcast station in the evening. Student participation consists of viewing the 45 half-hour broadcasts (for a three-unit course), completing reading assignments, and taking a mid-term and final examination on the campus he has elected. Each student has the privilege of attending voluntary seminars, and of consulting via telephone or in person with an instructor at the campus of registry during designated hours.

The consortium is considered a success by the participating institutions. In the words of a consortium handout: "Firemen, whose schedules often prohibit campus classes, can take televised courses. Mothers whose home responsibilities prevent their coming to campus are able to attend classes via television. And regular students whose campus class sections are closed are able to find room within the elastic walls of a televised course." In short, the program serves previously bypassed populations and regular students as well. Another consortium statement claims that these courses are not substitutional but, in fact, attract new students into the system: "Several semesters of experience have led us to the conclusion that there is no discernible decrease in on-campus enrollments when a course is televised. On the contrary, televised community college courses attract new students, who become acquainted with their community college through television." However, as noted earlier in this book (p. 67), there are recent indications that some new courses are leading to cancellation of on-campus course sections.

Little evaluation and research on the outcomes of consortium courses have been conducted, but some very cursory analyses indicate that performance of TV students is comparable to that of on-campus students. Questionnaire studies of students enrolled in two different courses at each of three different colleges led to the following generalizations about the TV students:

- Nearly one-half of the students are in the 20- to 30-year age bracket, with the remainder about equally divided between under 20s and older students. Two-thirds of those enrolling are women.
- About one-third of those enrolled classify themselves occupationally as students, and most have been regularly enrolled in school within the past two or three years. About one-fifth identify themselves as housewives.
- From 12 to 24 percent in the various programs have only a high school education or less.
- Close to one-third report incomes under $3,000 yearly (about the same proportion who identify themselves as students). One-sixth are in the over-$12,000 a year bracket, with the remaining half distributed over mid-income ranges in about the same way as the general population.
- From 30 to 40 percent report that they learned about the course in which they were enrolled through brochures which were mailed from or picked up at a college. Announcements on television and word-of-mouth each account for about 15 percent of the enrollments, and the remainder resulted from a variety of other sources.
- An analysis by one of the colleges of the grade distribution for the courses shows mixed results, suggesting no pattern of higher or lower grades for TV students. Off-campus students were much more likely to withdraw from a course, however—43 and 46 percent for two of the courses, whereas only 35 and 27 percent withdrew from similar on-campus courses.

Consortium courses are available to other institutions at a charge of $75 per half-hour segment for unlimited use during a semester. However, little active marketing has been undertaken. To date, only one course (art history) has been exported for use in the San Francisco area, where it was broadcast over a commerical station to an early morning audience of 225 enrolled students.

A Live, Interactive Television Course
by the Northern California ITV Consortium

The Northern California ITV Consortium was established in the fall of 1972 "to extend the effective service area of colleges and universities in Northern California . . . [in order to] serve the continuing education needs of all adults in the region." Part of the consortium's purpose is to enlarge the curricula of participating schools, but its primary aim is to extend educational services to persons not now reached by these institutions. The consortium, which is based at California State University at Sonoma, received a total of $70,000 for its first year from state funds and from the Title I program of the federal Higher Education Act.*

Under the direction of Dr. Stuart Cooney, the structure of this consortium is much less formalized than that of the Southern California Regional Consortium. There are no set guidelines for participation, and the courses it offers are intended to be experimental and innovative. Ultimately, the consortium hopes to include the six state universities, the two University of California campuses and the 34 community colleges in the region, but at present, the state universities are the most active participants. However, three community colleges have representatives on the consortium steering committee and faculty members from the University of California at Davis are participating as individuals in the planning of a

---

*The Title I federal program is specifically designated for the support of educational programs which contribute to solving community problems.

new course. Dr. Cooney is satisfied with this arrangement, since he believe that keeping the consortium structure as open as possible is the best way for it to grow.

The consortium's first course, "Health, Poverty and Public Policy," was offered via television in the spring of 1973. The purpose of the course is to inform and sensitize public officials to the health needs of the poor. The syllabus covers available health resources, assesses their quality, and explores the problems of the poor in gaining access to them. The target audience for the course was a wide range of state and local government officials, as well as private individuals involved in health-care and poverty programs (the head administrator of a group medical practice is one example). The course was taught by Dr. George D. Kent of the Department of Political Science at Chico State University. Dr. Kent had previously taught a classroom version of the course at Yuba College in Marysville as part of Chico State's extension service at three educationally isolated locations in Northern California—Marysville, Susanville, and Redding—and television seemed an attractive alternative for reaching a widely scattered audience. But Dr. Kent had had no previous experience with teaching by television, and he quickly learned that planning and preparation for the course required considerable amounts of his time and creative energies.

"Health, Poverty and Public Policy" was presented as a two-credit course on five Saturday mornings in Spring 1973. The course programs originated from Redding and were carried live over the educational television stations (linked by microwave) in Chico, Redding and Humboldt. The course was intended to be watched in groups and was structured to maximize active individual participation, both through local group discussions and through call-in questions. The three primary viewing sites at Marysville, Susanville, and Redding had paid moderators. In addition, other viewing sites were established wherever three or more enrolled students could be gathered. In these circumstances, one participant served as group leader. Considerable effort was put into the course promotion in order to reach the economic break-even point of 480 students.

The course budget was as follows:

Expenses

Instructional salaries (faculty, guests)	$ 2,700
Production expenses	3,000
Transmission costs 15 hours @ $125/hr.	1,875
Support personnel	1,000
Other support costs (travel)	565
Evaluation	1,760
Planning, development, promotion	9,000
	$ 19,900

Revenues

Federal funds	$	5,000
Direct consortium contribution		1,500
Student fees 480 @ $28		13,440
	$	19,940

Edu-Cable: A Proposed
Profit-Making Educational Cable Service

Business Plan Edu-Cable is a proposal for using leased cable channels to provide educational courses on a profit-making basis. The plan was developed by H. S. Dordick, the former Director of Telecommunications for the City of New York, for the President's Office of Telecommunications Policy. His plan, which represents only the author's thinking and is not an official OTP document, provides an extremely useful analysis of the economics of continuing education on cable and offers an interesting model for cooperation between educational institutions, cable operators and a private corporation. As described in the Foreword to the plan, it has been structured

> *as if it were to be used for an imminent entrepreneurial venture, possibly involving venture capital from the investment community. The intent is to demonstrate, if possible, sufficient economic viability to make Edu-Cable a reasonably attractive business risk, requiring little or no stimulation from governmental agencies (especially on an on-going basis) . . . . Apart from possible seed sponsorship, the concept of Edu-Cable is as a privately financed, entrepreneurial activity capable of being self-supporting in the commercial marketplace.*

The major features of the plan, in summary form, are as follows:

I. *Operating Assumptions*

A. The Edu-Cable Corporation (ECC) will provide adult and post-secondary courses over leased CATV channels. ECC will cooperate, not compete, with existing educational institutions. Courses disseminated by ECC will be sponsored, publicized and accredited by the originating institutions. Actual production may be done by either the institution or ECC.

B. All revenues to ECC are considered to derive from subscriber enrollment charges. Access to programming will be controlled through the use of "scrambled" pay-cable channels.

C. The plan is considered feasible only for systems with a minimum of 5,000 subscribers. Courses will be offered only if a minimum of 5 percent of system subscribers enroll.

D. To minimize production costs, first programs will be essentially taped classroom instruction. More elaborately produced courses will be offered as soon as possible, however.

II. *Operational Plan*

The "initial objective of ECC is to achieve profitable operations on at least one leased CATV channel within a two-year operating period." Three key factors in reaching this goal will be

(1) *Finding optimal sites.* A large CATV system in an area that also contains one or more successful extension services should offer the best potential market. An example of a suitable area for ECC is the West Los Angeles area, presently served by the Theta-Cable system, with 22,000 subscribers. UCLA is located in the same area and operates a large extension program.

(2) *Determining kinds and costs of programs.* The initial programs should be of wide interest but should not require elaborate production. A number of popular UCLA extension courses, such as "The Family in Transition" and "The Folksingers," are the kind of course contemplated.

(3) *Determining method and cost for providing access and charging for cablecast programs.* The plan assumes that ECC will charge on a *per-program* basis, utilizing available channel-access technology. Terminals would be placed in the homes of all CATV subscribers to permit "impulse buying." While these terminal costs may be shared with other pay-cable operators, the plan's financial projections assume total cost is borne by ECC.

III. *Marketing Plan*

The first stage of marketing would be a market-response survey of cable subscribers on a system under consideration by ECC. A second target market would be those who reside in the cable system's area but do not subscribe. The next stage would be an extensive campaign to publicize the ECC channel and its services. It is assumed that the educational institution and cable operator would cooperate in this effort, since both stand to gain by ECC's success. Additional cable channels could be leased in remote communities lacking comparable educational services. This would be desirable since it would increase the potential market without increasing production costs.

A key factor in the marketing plan involves the channel-access equipment. The optimal procedure would be to place access terminals in each home, sharing the costs with other pay-cable entrepreneurs. However, as noted, the plan's financial projections make the worst-case assumption that all costs will be borne by ECC.

IV. *Financial Projections*

A. All *revenues* are derived from subscriber charges, computed on the following assumptions:

(1) To be competitive with on-campus tuition, "charges of $1 per hour for non-credit viewing and $2 per hour for credit viewing are assumed. With a 50 percent mix of credit and non-credit, an average revenue of $1.50 per hour is achieved."

(2) " '100 percent Utilization' is defined as 20 hours of different programs a week . . . viewed and paid for by at least 5 percent of the CATV system's subscribers." Each program is repeated three times per week for viewer convenience, but only 20 hours are "billable."

(3) Revenues produced by ECC are given for systems of three different sizes, based on 50 weeks a year of programming:

CATV system	Size	Course subscribers (5% total)	ECC revenue/ hour	Yearly revenue 100% utilization
A	5,000	250	$ 375	$ 375,000
B	10,000	500	$ 750	$ 750,000
C	20,000	1,000	$1,500	$1,500,000

Dordick notes that these figures represent an average expenditure per CATV subscriber household of $75 per year or $6.25 per month, which "appears a very realizable goal at this time."

B. *Costs* are divided into six major categories and estimated as follows:

(1) *Channel leasing.* Maximum cost is assumed to be no more than 1/20th of the income of a 20-channel system. Assuming an average CATV subscription charge of $5 per month or $60 per year per subscriber, channel leasing costs for the three hypothetical systems would be

System	Total revenues/yr.	Lease cost/yr.	Lease cost/hr. (100% utilization)
A	$ 300,000	$15,000	$15
B	$ 600,000	$30,000	$30
C	$1,200,000	$60,000	$60

If only ten programs per week were offered (50 percent utilization), the lease cost per hour would, of course, be doubled.

(2) *Program production and copyright costs.* It is acknowledged that production costs can vary widely. Three general levels of production costs are estimated as $300 per hour for simple, black and white, production; $600 per hour for color production; and $1,200 per hour for more elaborate studio production. Amortized over four showings, production costs would be $75 per hour at the low end, $150 per hour for moderate production, and $300 per hour as the top range. The programs might be produced by either ECC or the sponsoring institution. In the latter case, the costs would be borne by that institution, and ECC would pay 50 percent of gross subscriber receipts for use of the material, which seems "a reasonable approximation." If ECC produces the programs, the sponsoring institution would receive only 25 percent of subscriber receipts as a royalty payment.

(3) *Capital facilities and operating costs.* These are estimated also on three levels, depending on whether ECC simply plays programming provided to it (Mode 1), has a mobile color-production capability (Mode 2a), or has its own color studio (Mode 2b). The capital costs are assumed to be amortized over four years; the operating costs cover technical personnel to operate the ECC channel:

Mode	Capital costs	Capital costs/hr.	Operating costs/yr.	Operating costs/hr.
1	$ 20,000	$ 5	$24,000	$24
2a	$ 80,000	$20	$54,000	$54
2b	$160,000	$40	$84,000	$84

(4) *Support costs.* This includes clerical costs, rent and utilities, office supplies, telephone, insurance, legal and accounting fees, promotional costs, and the salary of a general manager. These are estimated at 120 percent of the operating costs, or $30 per hour for Mode 1, $65 per hour for Mode 2a, and $100 per hour for Mode 2b.

(5) *Access control costs.* This covers the cost of purchasing and installing "de-scrambler" devices in the homes of potential ECC customers. A number of such devices are available now, but none have been produced in large quantities. Costs, though still uncertain, are estimated at $50 per subscriber. As noted earlier, it is assumed that a terminal will be installed in *every* subscriber's home, with the cost amortized over four years:

System	Total cost for terminals	Installment cost/yr.	Cost/billable hour (100% utilization)
A(5,000)	$ 250,000	$ 62,500	$ 62.50
B(10,000)	$ 500,000	$125,000	$125.00
C(20,000)	$1,000,000	$250,000	$250.00

V. *Break-even Projections*

The sum of all costs listed above are calculated per billable hour and are plotted against varying rates of utilization:

System	Mode	Break-even point
C – 20,000	1	70% utilization
C – 20,000	2b	80% utilization
A – 5,000	1	80% utilization
A – 5,000	2b	140% utilization

Thus, the most profitable mode of operation is to have programs produced by educational institutions (and pay them 50 percent of revenues). Only for larger systems does it appear feasible to have ECC produce programs. Otherwise, ECC seems workable for small (5,000 subscriber) systems only if program production is not necessary.

VI. *Profit and Loss Forecast*

Launching ECC would require pre-operating negotiations with a CATV operator for lease of a channel, with educational institutions for courses, and with an access-control equipment supplier for terminals. Cost of these negotiations is not counted in ECC's operating budget. ECC operations would begin with a six-month start-up period for production of courses, installation of terminals and promotion. After actual service begins, it is assumed ECC will operate at 25 percent utilization (billable hours/week) for the first three months, at 50 percent utilization for the next three months, and at 100 percent utilization thereafter. These forecasts show that

(1) ECC operating in a 20,000 subscriber system, with programs supplied by the educational institutions, would become profitable in the third quarter of the first year. Within 18 months of beginning operations, it would reach the cumulative break-even point, where total pre-tax profits equal initial start-up losses. Subsequent pre-tax profits would average over 25 percent of sales, which "indicates an excellent business profit."

(2) If ECC produced the programs on a 20,000 subscriber system, it would take almost two years to reach the cumulative break-even point. After the first two years, however, higher profits would be produced in this mode.

(3) For a 5,000 subscriber system, with programs produced by the institutions, the cumulative break-even point occurs at the end of almost three years of operation. Clearly, the prospects for risk are greater and the profit potentials lower for smaller systems.

Table 4 summarizes the financial analyses for the three hypothetical situations described above.

VII. *Risk and Sensitivity Analysis*

A. The plan is based on the presumption that adult interest in education is growing and that a typical CATV household will be willing to pay $75 per year for a variety of academic, arts and crafts, and vocational instruction. ECC may well be more successful in remote areas with little current access to continuing education.

B. Most channel leasing to date has been based on a percentage of gross revenues. Since ECC may be more risky than premium entertainment, operators may well want a flat payment from ECC. Although this requires a greater initial cost, it should make for higher profits in the long run.

C. "By far the most serious risk . . . is the cost of the program material itself." While it is assumed that ECC could begin with simple taped classroom instruction, this clearly will not be satisfactory for long-term success. The cost of conventional television production, even of modest quality, often runs $1,000 per minute of programming. The report concludes that "in this program production area, federal funding is not only necessary but sensible, at least initially while market response is being confirmed." The U.S. Office of Education is mentioned as a logical source of funds, as well as the Department of Labor for vocational education programs.

Table 4.
Financial Summary of Operation of One Edu-Cable Channel

Mode of operation	Start-up operation				Steady-state operation		
	Profitable Operations	Cumulative break-even point	Max-neg. cash flow	Cash flow crossover point	Annual revenues	Pre-tax profit	Return on investment
20,000-subscriber CATV system; EEC does not program production	9 mo.	20 mo.	$370,000	24 mo.	$1,500,000	$382,000	35%
20,000-subscriber CATV system; EEC does all program production	13 mo.	23 mo.	$540,000	28 mo.	$1,500,000	$434,000	37%
5,000-subscriber CATV system; EEC does not program production	14 mo.	32 mo.	$136,000	45 mo.	$ 375,000	$ 52,000	12%

Guidelines for the Application of
Technology to Educational Objectives

James Gibbons

We have known for some time that instructional technology has the potential to bring a much-needed revolution to education at all levels. In particular, a proper application of technology should enable us to remove many of the barriers to education that arise from age, sex, race, quality of prior education, learning style, family obligations, job responsibilities and so on. Technology can also help us solve the increasingly important problem of cost-effectiveness in education, which arises from the character of a system in which faculty serve in the multiple roles of teacher, researcher, tester and counselor.

We have already made some progress in using technology to reach these goals. However, our efforts in the past do not seem to have been based on an adequate formulation of the problem. For example, in the decade from 1960 to 1970, the federal government alone spent approximately $3 billion on "educational technology." This expenditure was largely to enable schools to purchase hardware, on the assumption that teachers would be able use use the hardware creatively in their teaching. But by and large these hopes did not materialize. Recent studies, of which the Carnegie Commission's *The Fourth Revolution* is only the newest, have noted this problem: ". . . the principal deficiency is in the availability of computer programs, video and audio tapes, printed learning modules, films and other 'software' of instructional technology." The Carnegie Commission proposes to overcome this problem by generating the software needed to assist teachers in the effective uses of technology.

To be specific, the commission and other groups have recommended a number of federally sponsored, cooperative learning-technology centers, an idea which would surely go a long way toward harnessing technology for educational purposes. However, while such centers would undoubtedly be very helpful for assuring greater penetration of technology in a number of educational enterprises, they still cannot guarantee that the video tapes and other software produced will make education either more effective or more accessible. Indeed, experience with the products of similar centers in the past has been that the use of such materials does not justify the cost of producing them. It is difficult to see how the solution proposed by the Carnegie Commission would clearly avoid this difficulty.

On the other hand, there are a number of very successful ventures in the use of technology in education. The table at the end of this piece describes six of the most important of these ventures in which radio and/or television is used as an open broadcast instructional medium. It is interesting to note that all but one of these ventures are outside the United States.

An analysis of both the successful ventures and some spectacular failures leads to a number of *common* program elements that form a set of guidelines for the successful application of technology. These guidelines are presented below with occasional commentary on specific points.

1. The educational program must be planned for a specific *target audience.*
2. *Specific educational objectives* that are relevant to the needs and interests of the target audience must be clearly understood and agreed on. These specific objectives may well include career education, but are certainly not limited to that. For example, education for social responsibility and to fulfill cultural interests are accepted goals of the British Open University.
3. A systematic *multi-media approach* must be used, and both knowledge specialists and media specialists should be employed in the production of material. It is especially interesting to note that where a particular institution or faculty member has persevered in the use of instructional technology, they have, over time, become much less committed to the dominant use of video technology and much more pleased with simpler schemes, such as audio tapes and coordinated slides. The ideal should be that an instructor would choose the correct medium for presenting a given concept as unconsciously as he chooses a ball point pen.
4. Educators who are capable of learning and using the *instructional characteristics* of various media must be found. This is perhaps a major bottleneck, for there are virtually no institutions that train people in this area.
5. Clear and careful provision for *personal interaction* (student-student, student-working colleague, student-faculty, etc.) must be made, since people are not self-correcting. Even in very successful applications of technology to education (*e.g.,* the first-year archaeology course at the University of California at Santa Barbara), it has been found that when personal interaction is removed, student interest and motivation rapidly disappear.
6. *Evaluation and feedback arrangements* must be used to monitor audience

reaction and to change the instructional material to suit audience needs.

These common elements define a systematic approach to educational technology. In particular, the use of evaluative feedback is central and will, if carefully applied, increase the probability of final success of the venture. In effect, the use of feedback tends to ensure that the programs will be self-correcting and self-renewing. However, reliance on a purely mechanistic approach will lead to mechanistic results, including even greater depersonalization than we find in our present educational system. It is therefore imperative that we look beyond results which claim, for example, that there is "no significant difference" in learning from television as opposed to conventional learning. We need to determine what the long-term effects of a greatly increased penetration of technology might be, and to support projects that recognize personal development and growth as being much more important than increased efficiency.

A further point that deserves careful elaboration relates to the amount of time that students spend with technological aids. As is suggested in the table below (see especially the column labeled "Teaching Format"), a very small amount of the total time that students spend studying a given course is spent watching television or listening to audio tapes or a radio. At the British Open University, for example, only about 5 percent of a student's time is occupied by TV and radio presentations. Another excellent example is the archaeology course at the University of California at Santa Barbara, where a week's work for a student (10-15 hours) includes one audio tape of approximately 1½ hours (which is used in conjunction with a carefully prepared study guide and 40 to 50 slides), one 50-minute lecture, one 50-minute seminar, 75-100 pages of reading, and one *optional* 20-minute video tape (which is used when it is desirable to show motion or to compress a time scale into a manageable length—for example, to illustrate the process by which stone erodes). Thus, the total student time spent using technological aids is less than 20 percent.

It is also interesting to note that even in cases where the original television programming was produced with only very generalized educational objectives, its application in a course for college credit involves much more background reading and class discussion than viewing time. A very creative college course on dramatic arts in television (offered by Ms. Brigitte Dobson at Chico State University in California) used the two BBC series "King Henry VIII" and "Elizabeth Rex," but the required student viewing occupied only 30 percent of the student's total time.

My principal conclusions:

1. Users of media centers, whether national or local, should follow the guidelines set out above to ensure effectiveness of the materials they produce.
2. We should not expect technology to dominate the learning process, but rather to facilitate it. In some cases technology may permit us to do the same thing we now do more cheaply; but its major contribution to cost-effectiveness will most likely be in providing much more effective education for less *additional* cost than other schemes we could contemplate.

Comparison of Six Television-Based Educational Programs

	NHK Gakuen (Japan)	Bavarian Telekolleg	TV Technical College (Poland)	Chicago TV College	British Open University	Australian Radio Correspondence School and School of the Air
Starting Date	1963	1967	1966	1956	1971	1933 & 1951
Principal Objectives	1. Upgrade labor force 2. Offer high school to those who did not attend.	Alternate route to trade or technical school diploma.	1. Enrich corresponding study of employed students. 2. Reduce necessity of traveling to schools.	Bring two-year college to persons unable to study on campus.	1. Expand opportunities for higher education. 2. Provide B.A. for persons with less than A-level qualifications, *if* they can succeed.	Provide education for children who live in remote areas. Also available to prisoners.
Organization	Independent institution with government charter. National TV network supplies 90% of budget. 100 teachers, 250 part-time readers of correspondence.	Jointly operated by state of Bavaria and Bayerische Rundfunk. State provides schools and administration for group study, corrects and grades written work, gives exams.	Jointly operated by Ministry of Education and Polish Radio and Television.	Operated by department of Chicago City College. CCC has a number of campuses that provide teachers. Broadcasts produced and transmitted by local public TV station.	Royal charter with usual academic and administrative departments, but special arrangements for broadcasting and handling correspondence study. 280 study centers scattered throughout Britain.	Separate states maintain and administer correspondence schools; Australian Broadcasting Corp. responsible for radio courses. Summer camp for all students.
Types of Students and Enrollment Data	50% working, 60% living at home. 51% teenage, 30% in 20s, 10% in 30s. Enrollment: Peaked at 18,626 in 1968; estimated at 17,000 for 1971.	81% working, 80% under 35. Primarily for elementary school graduates. Enrollment averages 8,500 per year.	90% men, 50% outside cities. Registration about 12,000 per year; open to anyone eligible for higher technical training. Many students lack qualifications to enter full time.	75% women, 67% in 20s and 30s. Enrollment: about 7,000 for credit; 4,000 non-credit. 600 full-time equivalent.	Must be over 21. Selection based on area quota and likelihood of success. Enrollment among occupational groups in first year: teachers—34%; professions and arts—9.7%; housewives—9.6%; scientists & engineers (with B.A.)—9.1%; lab assistants & techs—9.1%; clerical & office staff—8%; administrators & managers—5%; shop keepers, sales service, recreation workers—37%; trades, not working & armed forces—10%. Total enrollment limit (34,000) current enrollment—25,000.	Largely children in primary school age group. In New South Wales, enrollment was 6,800 in 1966 and 6,000 in 1970. Of the 6,000, 400 were prisoners.
Curriculum	25 courses covering general high school curriculum. Specialized courses for home economics and factory work.	14 courses, five required of all students (German, English, algebra & geometry, history, physics). Students going on to technical schools take biology, drawing, economics, electrical engineering and bookkeeping.	17 existing colleges register students for both residence classes and correspondence work. Course is four years long, with first two taken by correspondence.	Standard two-year college curriculum. Social science, biology, physics, humanities, and English composition required of everyone.	Starting Jan. 1971 OU offered 4 foundation courses in humanities, social sciences, mathematics, and natural sciences. Larger number of increasingly specialized courses in 2nd, 3rd, & 4th years. Candidate for B.A. must pass 6 courses, including 2 foundation courses. B.A. with honors must pass 8 courses.	Standard curriculum of state schools. However, some secondary and even university-level work is provided.

Teaching Format	Chiefly correspondence, with one TV program per week. Gakuen staff makes texts, exercise books. Students *required* to take full course, finishing 3 years of high school in 4 years. 3 exams per year plus final.	Each course has 78 lessons, with one TV program per lesson. Also home exercises, readings, correspondence. Access to recorded cassettes for language study by telephone. Every 3rd week a student must attend Day College for 5 hours.	2½ hours of TV per week on math, chemistry, and physics in 1st year. Also math, physics, strength of materials, and EE second year. Polish factories close at 4 PM. Broadcasts begin at 3 PM.	TV transmission 26 hours/week, 45-minute broadcasts per course per week. Correspondence and on-campus study available but not required. Exams given on campus.	Each course taught by team of knowledge and media specialists. Each course includes text, exercises for computer marking, correspondence assignments. 36 TV and 36 radio broadcasts. TV is illustrated lecture, radio for discussion of difficulties raised by students. Only about 5% of total time occupied by TV and radio. Students expected to spend 10 hours week per course.	Chiefly correspondence materials and assignments sent to children, returned for grading. State furnishes desks and visiting teacher where enough children can be congregated. Otherwise mother is teacher, and some radio broadcasts are for mother-teachers. Flying doctors provide two-way radio service for questions, discussions, etc.
Cost to Students	Approximately $25/year.	Approximately $50 for entire course of study.	No cost for TV. Other costs not available.	$75 per course plus cost of texts.	$24 registration fee, $108 for each foundation course, $48 for each upper level. Total for regular B.A.: $432.	No fees for lessons, materials, postage, etc.
Graduation Statistics	25% of entrants.	25% of all entrants.	Not available.	To date, 300 students have taken all work for A.A. degree by TV; about 1,900 have completed at least 1 semester. 75% of registrants complete courses and receive degrees.	1st year: 25,000 accepted, and 16,000 passed exams at end of first year. Large proportion did *not* have A-level qualification. No B.A. graduates expected until 1976.	No data available.
Operating Costs	TV programming— $2500/hr. Radio programming— $260/hr.	TV production— $10,000/hr. Unit costs lower than normal schools.	Not available.	Average budget is about $550,000/year, with 43% for studio time and videotaping.	About $15 million budgeted for development. $7.5 million spent so far. Cost of 5,000 student residence university, for comparison, would be about $40 million. First year operating costs were $3.6 million for TV and radio production and transmission, $6.5 million for direct student expenses.	Estimated at $367/student in New South Wales in 1967.
Remarks	NHK now broadcasting pilot courses in Tokyo and Osaka for home university study, expecting to establish open university in about 2 years.	About $5 million spent in research, planning, development, etc., between the years 1966-1969. Annual budget averaged $1 million/ year for first four years but projected to be $250,000 per year.	1. *Any* person in Poland can take end-of-year exams for 1st year's study. If they pass, they can formally enter one of the technical colleges. 2. Research indicates that students who use broadcasts do better than those who don't. 3. Facilities used for children's education in the morning.	1. Careful comparisons of performances between TV students and campus students show that TV students learn as well or better than campus students. 2. With 600 full-time students, budget is $900/ year per student, which is lower than on-campus cost (and could be *much* lower if TV enrollment increased to 3,000 full-time students).		Anecdotal evidence indicates that children who have completed primary school by correspondence do well when they go away to a secondary boarding school.

Abstracts

Learning from Television: What the Research Says

by Godwin G. Chu and Wilbur Schramm

Summary of major observations from the report, "Learning from Television: What the Research Says." This is the result of a study by the Institute for Communication Research, Stanford University, for the U.S. Office of Education, 1967.

I. Do pupils learn from television?
1. Given favorable conditions, children learn efficiently from instructional television.
2. By and large, instructional television can more easily be used effectively for primary and secondary school students than for college students.
3. So far as we can tell from present evidence, television can be used efficiently to teach any subject matter where one-way communication will contribute to learning.

II. What have we learned about the efficient use of instructional television in a school system?
4. Television is most effective as a tool for learning when used in a suitable context of learning activities at the receiving end.
5. Television is more likely to be an efficient part of an educational system when it is applied to an educational problem of sufficient magnitude to

call forth broad support.

6. Television is more likely to be an efficient tool of learning if it is planned and organized efficiently.

III. What have we learned about the treatment, situation, and pupil variables?

7. There is no evidence to suggest that either visual magnification or large-size screen will improve learning from television in general.

8. There is insufficient evidence to suggest that color will improve learning from film or television.

9. Where learning of perceptual-motor skills is required, a subjective angle presentation on television will tend to be more effective than an objective angle presentation.

10. There is no clear evidence on the kind of variations in production techniques that significantly contribute to learning from instructional television. However, students will learn better when the visuals are presented in a continuous order and carefully planned both by the television team and the studio teacher.

11. Attention-gaining cues that are irrelevant to the subject matter will most probably have a negative effect on learning from instructional television.

12. There is no consistent evidence to suggest that either humor or animation significantly contributes to learning from instructional television.

13. Subtitles tend to improve learning from instructional television, particularly when the original program is not well organized.

14. There is insufficient evidence to suggest that dramatic presentation will result in more learning than will expository presentation in instructional television.

15. Inserting questions in a television program does not seem to improve learning, but giving the students a rest pause does.

16. Whether a television program is used to begin or to end a daily lesson by the classroom teacher makes no difference in learning.

17. Repeated showings of a television program will result in more learning, up to a point. But a teacher-directed follow-up, where available, is more effective than a second showing of the same program.

18. If saving time is important, a television program can probably be shortened and still achieve the minimum requirement of teaching.

19. There is no clear evidence to suggest whether eye-contact in television instruction will affect the amount of learning.

20. Problem-solving instruction on television is more effective than lecturing where the materials taught involve the solving of a problem.

21. The students are likely to acquire the same amount of learning from instructional television whether the materials are presented as a lecture, or in an interview, or in a panel discussion.

22. Where accurate perception of images is an important part of learning, wide viewing angle and long distance will interfere with learning from instructional television.

23. Adequate attention provided by the classroom teacher will, in most cases at least, remedy the adverse effect due to a wide viewing angle.

24. Noise will reduce the effectiveness of learning from film and television so far as part of the learning comes from the auditory medium.

25. Instructional television appears to be equally effective with small and large viewing groups.

26. Instructional television may or may not be more effective with homogeneously grouped students, depending on other factors in the learning situation.

27. Whether instructional television can teach students who view at home as effectively as students in the classroom seems to depend on other conditions.

28. At the college level, permissive attendance does not seem, by itself, to reduce the effectiveness of instructional television.

29. Students will learn more from instructional television under motivated conditions than under unmotivated conditions.

30. Learning from television by the students does not seem necessarily to be handicapped by the lack of prompt feedback to the instructor.

31. Showing, testing, revising an instructional television program will help substitute for lack of live feedback to the teacher and make for more learning by the students.

32. The lack of opportunity for students to raise questions and participate in free discussion would seem to reduce the effectiveness of learning from instructional television, particularly if the students are fairly advanced or the material is relatively complicated.

33. If a student being taught by instructional television can be given immediate knowledge of whether he has responded correctly, he will learn more.

34. Students taught by television tend to miss the personal teacher-student contact, but there is insufficient evidence to suggest that the lack of such contact will impair learning from instructional television.

35. Practice, whether by overt or covert response, will improve learning from instructional television if the practice is appropriate to the learning task, and if the practice does not constitute an interference.

36. Note-taking while viewing instructional television is likely to interfere with learning if time for it is not provided in the telecast.

IV. Attitudes toward instructional television.

37. Teachers and pupils are more favorable toward the use of instructional television in elementary school than in secondary school and college.

38. Administrators are more likely to be favorable toward instructional television than are teachers.

39. Voluntary home students of televised college classes tend to be more favorable toward learning by television than are the students who take these same televised courses in the classroom.

40. At the college level, students tend to prefer small discussion classes to television classes, television classes to large lecture classes.

41. There is evidence of a Hawthorne effect among students beginning to use

instructional television, but no firm evidence that attitudes toward the medium necessarily improve or worsen with time.

42. Favorable attitudes are distributed widely enough among different televised courses to cast doubt on the assumption that some academic subjects, per se, may be disliked as material for instructional television.

43. Liking instructional television is not always correlated with learning from it.

44. Among the factors that determine teachers' attitudes toward instructional television are (a) how they perceive the degree of threat to the classroom; (b) how they estimate the likelihood of mechanized instruction replacing direct contact with students; (c) how they estimate the effectiveness of instructional television; (d) the difficulties they see in the way of using modern techniques; (e) how conservative they are, and whether they trust or distrust experimentation.

45. Among the factors that determine pupils' attitudes toward instructional television are (a) how much contact they think they will have with a teacher; (b) how they compare the relative abilities of the studio and classroom teachers; (c) whether they find instructional television boring or interesting; (d) the nature of the televised programs they have seen; (e) the conditions of viewing.

V. Learning from television in developing regions.

46. There is no evidence to lead us to believe that children learn any less efficiently from television in developing countries than elsewhere.

47. Under suitable conditions, television has been shown to be capable of highly motivating learning in developing regions.

48. Illiterate people need to learn certain pictorial conventions. There is some evidence suggesting that these conventions are not hard to learn.

49. When media are introduced for upgrading the level of instruction, then it has proved very important to train teachers in their proper use and to keep in close touch with them.

50. Resistance to television and other media is likely to be no less in developing countries, but the size and urgency of the problems are likely to provide greater incentive for overcoming it.

51. Feedback from the classroom teacher to the studio teacher will be helpful to the effective use of the media.

52. There is ample evidence that the new media, particularly television, are effective for in-service training of teachers for developing regions.

VI. Learning from television: Learning from other media.

53. Given favorable conditions, pupils can learn from any instructional media that are now available.

54. There appears to be little if any difference between learning from television and learning from film, if the two media are used the same way.

55. Television and radio have certain advantages over films in flexibility and deliverability.

56. Radio is less expensive than television; economy of scale usually governs cost comparisons of television and film.

57. More complete control of film by the classroom teacher gives it a potential advantage over television.

58. The use of visual images will improve learning of manual tasks, as well as other learning where visual images can facilitate the association process. Otherwise, visual images may cause distraction and interfere with learning.

59. There is some evidence to suggest that moving visual images will improve learning if the continuity of action is an essential part of the learning task.

60. Student response is effectively controlled by programmed methods, regardless of the instructional medium.

The Medium May Be Related to the Message—College Instruction by TV

by Robert Dubin and R. Alan Hedley

Center for the Advanced Study of Educational Administration, University of Oregon, 1969.

This monograph is an attempt to establish research-based conclusions regarding the feasibility and consequences of the college-level utilization of educational television. The statistical analysis is organized around three distinct questions: (1) Can we distinguish the consequence of students taught by ETV from the consequences achieved by other media and methods of instruction? (2) Is there a systematic way in which the attitudes of college professors relate to the possibility that they may have to utilize ETV in their teaching? (3) Is there a special student reaction to being taught by ETV when compared with their reaction to the instructional technologies replaced by television instruction?

Through the use of statistical comparisons, the authors reach the following conclusions: Face-to-face instruction seems to have a general advantage over ETV when one compares the test results of students taught by the two methods. This is due to the distinct inferiority of two-way TV instruction which, perhaps by trying to be live—to replicate another medium—fails to get across its instructional content. By comparison, one-way ETV is just as good as face-to-face teaching by lecturing, by a combination of lecturing and discussion or demonstration, or even by discussion alone. Neither variations in teaching methods nor subjects taught affect this conclusion.

This means that university administrators are faced with a highly visible technical innovation, the intended consequences of which are neither better nor worse than the technology it replaces. Thus, what is needed is a framework for making educational decisions regarding the utilization of this new technology that treats the issue as one of technical innovation rather than educational policy change.

In this context, the attitudes of both users and consumers may make the single most important difference in whether the innovation will be adopted successfully or not. On the whole, students seem willing to accept ETV if the content and quality of instruction is of average or better quality. As students gains experience with televised instruction they probably will come to expect it as a normal feature of their instructional environment.

Although professors seem to be in favor of ETV in a general, diffuse way, the closer it gets to involving them personally, the more threatened they generally feel. Resistance seems to be strongest from individual faculty members who insist on the necessity of direct faculty-student contact—both as a mandatory part of the educational experience and, the authors speculate, as insurance against their own "redundancy" or technological unemployment.

However, the implication of individualized opposition is that no broad consensus is required among a faculty in order to initiate and continue to utilize ETV. Those who do not consider it a desirable innovation should not be forced to subscribe to its use, but college administrators should encourage the commitment of those faculty members who are willing to experiment by offering—as a start—the following incentives: an appropriate valuation of the increased teaching load represented; an equitable solution to the problem of replaying videotapes; an assurance that their academic freedom will not be transgressed; an absorption of non-TV professors displaced energies into research functions. Regardless of faculty reception, the fact is that today the quality of faculty instruction cannot keep up with increasing student enrollments. If ETV is viewed as a new means of distribution rather than a change in educational policy, and if faculty resistance can be overcome on an individual basis, it can be a very effective means of reaching large numbers of students with minimum additional faculty investments.

Three Models for
Home-Based Instructional Systems Using Television

by Rudy Bretz

The Rand Corporation Report #R-1089-USOE/MF, October 1972.

This is the final report of a brief study commissioned by the U.S. Office of Education which sought an analysis of the key elements of several successful instructional projects using home-based television. Their hope was to invest in a new nationwide program on career education for women contained in an entertainment format. Accordingly, the report presents for comparison three case studies: Chicago's TV College and Bavaria's "Telekolleg"—offering credit course programs on the junior college and secondary levels, respectively—and the Children's Television Workshop series, "Sesame Street"—basically an entertainment series for children, with a strong instructional emphasis. The report attempts to analyze these projects in terms of the planning and development elements that the author considers significant in the development of a general television instructional model. It does not venture into the area of relative effectiveness since it was assumed that as these projects continue in operation, they satisfy the goals for which they were intended.

Although all three case-study programs required similar activities in the preplanning and production stages of development prior to operational status, they varied widely in their strategies, objectives, methods, and scale of operations.

TV College, now in its 17th year, is a formal instructional service, programming about five hours a day over one local Chicago educational television broadcasting station. The service is aimed at adults in the metropolitan area seeking junior college degrees, course credits, or simply knowledge and skills. Currently about 500 credit and non-credit students are reached by each program, as well as an estimated 30,000 unregistered general-interest viewers. TV College is built on the facilities and resources, and it uses the faculty and educational program, of the City Colleges of Chicago. A Dean of Television Instruction is responsible for planning, policy-formation, and the overall direction of the program. All requirements except classroom attendance are the same for all students—televison or on-campus. Other elements beyond the television lessons classify this as a multimedia system. These include: a printed Teleclass Study Guide (containing a synopsis of each lesson, a summary of the major points, lists of required and collateral readings, assignments, and due dates); student homework assignments sent in by mail; telephone or personal contact with the TV or section instructor; midterms and final examinations taken at a local campus in conventional fashion; and text and reference books as appropriate.

The initial planning phase of TV College in 1956 took scarcely three months. During this period, arrangements were made to purchase television time, TV instructors were recruited and selected, a promotion campaign was begun, and the TV courses and the Teleclass Study Guide were prepared. Only in the past three years have course programs been prerecorded; previously they were transmitted live. Planning is an on-going function at TV College. Of the 18 courses currently being offered each year, seven are new and eleven are repeated, with updating as needed. While updating can be done over the summer, new courses are generally prepared during the school year, when the television instructor is assigned full-time to the TV College.

TV College is publicized widely throughout the Chicago metropolitan area. Information derived from both internal and external evaluation programs is used in the planning of new course offerings and in the modification of presentation techniques. Data from these surveys include: the size and composition of the viewing audience; aspects of the programs that are most attractive to the enrolled audience; and comparisons of the educational effectiveness of TV courses with that of similar courses taught by conventional methods. Based on the findings of comprehensive research into audience characteristics, TV College now intends to expand its programming to include special interest groups, such as those with deficiencies in basic literary skills and those with special occupational needs and interests.

Current operating budgets run from $850,000 to $900,000 annually, divided approximately among three categories as follows: (1) $300,000 for station operations; (2) $275,000 for teacher salaries; (3) about $250,000 for all other operations, including TV College staff, overhead, and equipment purchases.

"Telekolleg," now beginning its sixth year, is a formal instructional service of which television programming is a minor part, programming almost two hours daily over a network of transmitters covering the West German state of Bavaria. The service is aimed at home-based learners at the secondary school level interested in taking vocational courses leading eventually to a state-administered examination roughly equivalent to an American high school diploma. Nearly 10,000 credit students participate during a typical year, plus some 37,000 non-credit students. Unregistered general-interest viewers are estimated at 300,000 to 400,000. More than a series of television lessons, "Telekolleg" is a multi-media instructional system of interrelated components with excellent printed materials and group meetings for instructor-student and student-student interaction every third week. In this system, television programs and their development use no more than one-third the resources of the system. Lessons are produced by a creative television network staff with 20 years of experience in planning, producing, scheduling, and budgeting.

Although pre-planning needs were filled by the ongoing survey activity of the Bavarian Broadcasting System, specific planning and fund raising for Telekolleg took six months. An advisory council of some 14 persons was appointed to discuss and establish policy for "Telekolleg" and to give all interested institutions a part in the project. An agreement was formulated between the state and "Telekolleg," specifying the responsibilities of each. The production phase of the project involved several teams of eight to fifteen people. Composed of subject-matter specialists, teaching-method specialists, the TV editor, writers, and free-lance graphics designers, each team was responsible for planning the lessons in a single subject.

Promotion has been through newspaper advertisements, short TV "commercials," and mailed promotional announcements. "Telekolleg" works closely with several institutes that devote substantial effort to research and evaluation; their work provides the program's planners and producers with excellent feedback in such areas as analysis of student population and effectiveness of instructional method.

"Telekolleg's" ongoing annual budget totals about $326,000 per year. Officials report that "Telekolleg students cost the state one-sixth of the sum spent so far by traditional methods of schooling to provide pupils with a similar standard of qualification."

"Sesame Street" is now in its fourth year of operation. It is a general viewing, entertainment, and instructional series, programming one hour daily over some 250 stations nationwide. It is aimed at 3, 4, and 5-year-old pre-school children of the inner city as a special audience. The show's producers estimated an average daily viewing audience of 5-6 million children during the first year and as many as 8 million children by the middle of the second year. The CTW staff numbers nearly 200 workers, grouped by functions into nine departments. Informal working relationships between research and production staffs are reinforced by structured devices that ensure continued mutual understanding and cooperation. CTW also uses advisory panels of educators, psychologists, and other experts to help with the formulation of program objectives, and to review the progress of the development effort. Few non-television elements are used in the informal instruction of "Sesame Street." Those printed materials that were prepared are primarily for teacher and parent use or are promotional in nature.

During the pre-planning stage, the nucleus of the staff was brought together, the final selection of the Board of Advisors and Consultants was made, and a tentative developmental and operational model was adopted. During the planning stage, the staff defined basic instructional goals for the programs which were translated by the research staff into behavioral and operational terms. As a guide to production planning, the research staff both reviewed existing data and performed original research in order to determine the competence of the target audience in various curriculum areas. On the basis of research staff findings and recommendations, the production staff decided how much time to allot to each curriculum goal during each show, and writers produced scripts designed around these goals. Individual show segments were pre-tested before target audience samples to determine their educational effectiveness.

A major public relations firm was hired to assist in extensive audience promotion and to campaign for local program use. CTW augmented the professional firm's efforts with a door-to-door campaign to ensure audience use of the show and of the collateral materials. CTW also launched a utilization program intended to organize viewing groups and to reinforce the instructional goals of the program. Thirdly, a CTW field-service staff in each of fourteen major cities where broad-based community advisory councils and viewing center had been created was established. Feedback to the field-services staff as well as summative evaluation studies are channeled back to the CTW research and production staff and contribute to continuous modification and refinement of show material. CTW spent about $7.2 million from the spring of 1968 to the completion of one full season of broadcasting in June 1970.

Four other factors contributed to CTW's success: operations began with a clear idea of target audience and educational goals; the staff enjoyed the benefits of strong personal leadership; planning and production were relatively free from the usual deadlines that frequently limit the degree of preparation; and the field of children's programming was without any real competition.

From his comparison of the ways in which the three projects conducted their developmental stages, the author is able to conclude with a checklist of activities that are generally essential to the success of home-based instructional systems using television. The factors he lists include: during the pre-planning stage, the need for extensive formative research, including a specific definition of the target audience, its needs, level of motivation, general ability, background skills, and various living and viewing habits; and secondly, the need to establish a complexity and cost level for production and to identify personnel, community and funding resources. What is considered appropriate in style and complexity of production techniques will vary substantially, depending on whether the program uses direct instruction, is tied to an established degree-granting or skill-training system, and has a motivated target audience; or whether it is intended for general viewing competing with entertainment TV programming.

The above factors will determine the length of the planning period during which curriculum must be formulated, optimum methods and media must be chosen, staffs must be organized and trained, budget and appropriate air-time schedules must be ascertained, and formative and summative evaluation techniques must be selected.

Another important factor is the need for a carefully prepared and timed "promotional" campaign to inform the target audience of the date, time, and channel of the broadcast programs, and in the case of credit courses, how to enroll and obtain the printed materials. Further, market strategy must analyze target audience characteristics and then plan a marketing campaign by means of some of the following techniques: (1) direct advertising by TV, press, and radio; (2) cooperation of community leaders, local, state, or federal agencies; (3) a media public relations effort, including such activities as participation in radio and TV interview shows and supplying information to columnists; (4) direct mail approaches; (5) special grass-roots campaigns and personal contacts. The promotional activities and the public relations effort must peak about the time the program goes on the air.

Regardless of the amount of program production completed before operations begin, there is still a requirement for a certain amount of ongoing production as part of the operations phase, that is, for revision, replacement, or expansion of scheduled offerings. Other important activities in the operation of any instructional system using television are the organization of viewers and viewing groups and the maintenance of constant direct contact with the learner population.

Finally, an ongoing evaluation program must be adequately planned in advance. This program must include formative evaluation, aimed at improving the program effectiveness during the development and early operational stages, and summative evaluation, aimed at measuring the effectiveness of the project after its completion in terms of its success in achieving its objectives.

It is the author's implied conclusion that a career-education version of "Sesame Street" would not be a guaranteed success.

The Fourth Revolution—
Instructional Technology in Higher Education

Carnegie Commission on Higher Education

McGraw-Hill, June 1972.

The potential impact of new electronics is bringing higher education face-to-face with the first great technological revolution in five centuries. Traditional institutions can no longer adequately respond to society's demands that its ever-expanding variety of interests and objectives be accommodated. Yet, to date, educational changes are largely ad hoc, advancing unsystematically in response to the enthusiasms and achievements of scattered individuals. Although new technological developments have already transformed research techniques and administrative methods on many campuses, and are now affecting large libraries and instructional processes, they are coming along slowly, costing more money and adding to rather than replacing old technologies.

Nevertheless, the commission feels that instructional technology may provide the single greatest opportunity for academic changes on and off campus. For students, technology will offer greater access, flexibility, and variety in the learning experience. For faculty, technology will lessen routine instructional responsibilities and will lead to instruction that is more analytical in its approach, more conscious in its methods. For the general population, technology will offer new uses of leisure time, new job-training skills and the possibility of improved community interaction. What is needed is the integration of new media, long-familiar technology, the planning of instructional space, learning theories, and the professor into an organized total learning environment. As one advocate has stated, "Educational technology is not a bag of mechanical tricks, but the organized design and implementation of learning systems, taking advantage of, but not expecting miracles from, modern communications methods, visual aids, classroom organization and teaching methods." (J. R. Gass, Centre for Education Research and Innovation (CERI) 1971, p. 7.)

Although electronic devices may provide a solution to the conflicting needs of a widening student body, they must not be adopted merely because they exist. Overdevelopment of technology for relatively limited objectives could complicate the ultimate integration of technology into well-developed teaching and learning systems. To preserve the humanistic qualities of the educational process and to generate confidence in technology, these devices should be used only when (1) the teaching-learning task is critical to the course of instruction to which it is applied, and (2) the task could not be performed as well by other means. Caution also will be fostered naturally by low penetration: instructional software is not uniformly welcomed; hardware components are often incompatible; and program quality and individual expertise vary widely. Based on his general findings, one surveyor has concluded that "only those technologies well within the current state of the art are foreseen by faculty as destined for adoption within the next

15 years."

The commission report gives a brief review of the instructional technologies presently available in the following areas: multi-media classrooms, including routine audio-visual techniques; self-instruction units, including language labs, audio-listening centers, individual learning labs, and remote access units; instructional radio and television, including broadcast, closed circuit, cable, and videocassette programming; and computer-assisted instruction, including simulations, gaming, and computer-aided course design. The report then describes briefly how technology has figured in the efforts of several countries—Sweden, Japan, Great Britain, and West Germany—to extend educational opportunities to parts of their populations that formerly had to forego university education in order to earn a living.

The commission report also describes how technology will affect libraries. In the process of adjusting to geometrically increasing information, greater client demands and more complexity in the interrelations of concepts, libraries have made their own innovative uses of new electronic media. Through miniaturization processes, the use of computers for information retrieval, and the possibility of networking, libraries will come to play an increasingly important role in the community as focal learning centers for both formal and informal education.

The commission devotes the remainder of its report to the following recommendations:

Recommendation I

A case must be made for *early action* in the utilization of currently available technologies because: (1) learning experiences will become richer, more flexible, and more based on individual needs; (2) enormous investments already made in experimentation and research with technology are waiting to be utilized; (3) high short-run costs will greatly increase the productivity and efficient dispersal of instructional units; (4) if faculty resources can be invested now in the development and introduction of instructional programs using expanded technologies, the need to expand physical facilities and faculties in the future will be reduced; (5) coordination and planning for the use of instructional technologies will be easier now when considerable flexibility still exists than later when current directions become fixed. Technology should be encouraged by the adequate commitment of higher education to its utilization and development and by adequate support from governmental and other concerned agencies.

Recommendation II

The major thrust of *financial support* for instructional technology during the next decade should be to increase penetration through the development and utilization of outstanding existing programs suitable for use by more than one institution.

Recommendation III

Higher education especially must make an institutional commitment to a full and effective use of instructional technology by placing responsibility for its introduction and utilization at the highest possible levels of *academic administration*.

Recommendation IV

Improvement of *library services* must be given first priority.

Recommendation V

Extramural educational systems will play an early and crucial role in the ultimate development of instructional technology because their characteristics—they are free from tradition, they must develop materials that are largely self-instructing, they have no physical boundaries, and they are not subject to time restraints— imply a tolerance to innovation that makes them excellent testing grounds. Success here will challenge traditional institutions to attempt more innovation. Therefore, funding requests of these systems should be given favorable consideration.

Recommendation VI-VIII

Rather than favoring either government domination of or individual efforts at technological development, the commission recommends that at least seven cooperative "learning-technology centers," voluntarily organized on a regional basis by participating higher educational institutions should be established by 1992. The purpose of these systems should be to share costs and facilities for the accelerated development, acquisition, and utilization of instructional programs designed for use with expanded media. Although each learning-technology center should make use of existing developed libraries, computing, communications, and extramural instructional networks as part of its endeavors, the physical location of these various components can be dispersed. Initiative for the formation of these centers might be taken by individual institutions and states, existing computer, communications, or library networks or by regional educational associations. These centers would be service units for particpating institutions. Although they could engage in research and development activities, they would serve primarily as regional clearing-houses for the identification, production and distribution of information about the availability and use of new instructional materials. They would provide professional expertise and serve as a link between faculty members, government, foundations and industry. Each cooperative center would be divided up into production, resource, distribution and computing units. Funding would be provided by the federal government (which would provide all initial capital expenses and at least 1/3 of the operating costs during the first decade of operations); by participating institutions, student fees, and short-term special-project support from government, foundations, and industry. The estimated costs of one center are $35 million as an initial capital investment and $150 million in annual operating expenses. Operating authority should be entrusted to an individual director assisted by a relatively small committee of people representative of the main types of institutions involved. Wherever possible, existing facilities of participating institutions should be utilized.

Recommendation IX

The *federal government* should continue to provide a major share of expenditures required for research and development in instructional technology and for the introduction of new technologies into higher education. Increasing emphasis should be placed on supporting projects that will result in the actual production and increased utilization of new learning materials. *Granting agencies* should provide encouragement for the production of materials that can be widely used or readily adapted.

Recommendation X

The proposed *National Foundation of Post-Secondary Education,* with responsibility for administering loans and providing capital investment funds and grants for the utilization of instructional technology, and the proposed *National Institute of Education,* with responsibility for providing grants for research and development, should be established.

Recommendations XI-XII

Beginning in the 1980s, the effective utilization of instructional technology should have matured to the extent that greater numbers of students can be taught with fewer *faculty members.* The new role faculty will have to fill will be that of "a master of learning, at last afforded time and opportunity for the cultivation of students as individual human beings with a potential to learn." Professors must also become leaders of teams of instructional development personnel. Therefore, universities that are responsible for the training of prospective teachers should begin now to offer instruction on the development of teaching-learning segments that appropriately utilize the expanding technologies of instruction. Universities should also provide incentives to faculty members to contribute to the advancement in instructional technology through released time and salary improvements.

Recommendation XIII

Colleges and universities should supplement their instructional staffs with *qualified media technologists and information specialists* to assist instructors in the design, planning and evaluation of teaching-learning units that can be used with the expanding instructional technologies. Institutions of higher education at all levels should develop their potentials for training these specialists and professionals.

Recommendation XIV

Students will need to become versed in new skills in order to derive the most benefit from these developments. Therefore, high schools that do not already do so should offer instruction in basic concepts and *uses of computers* and should encourage their students to obtain, as early as possible, other skills that will be helpful in the use of new media for learning.

Recommendation XV

It has been difficult to assess the *costs of instructional technology* for the following reasons: (1) patterns of technology utilization differ from institution to institution; (2) there are considerable economic differences between the impact of the mere availability and the actual use of instructional technology by a campus; (3) much of the available cost data is for elementary and secondary education only; (4) researchers have been forced to use hypothetical models with built-in assumptions which may not be realized in actual use; (5) no allowances are made for decreases in certain costs as technology becomes more widely used; (6) the anticipated nature of institutional utilization of a given medium may be different from the actual use; and (7) there have been relatively few technology-wide cost studies that involve more than one medium.

An independent commission, supported either by an appropriate agency of the United States Department of Health, Education and Welfare or by one or more foundations, should be created to make assessments of the instructional effectiveness and cost benefits of currently available instructional technology. Findings of the commission should be published and appropriately disseminated for the advice of institutions of higher education, such cooperative learning-technology centers as may be established, and governments and foundations supporting the advancement of instructional technology.

Goals:

The Carnegie Commission suggests that the following goals be reached by 1980:

1. Institutions of higher learning will have accepted a broad definition of instructional technology such as: the enrichment and improvement of the conditions in which human beings learn and teach; achieved through the creative and systematic organization of resources, physical arrangements, media, and methods.

2. Most colleges and universities will have devised adequate administrative and academic authority and procedures for the encouragement and appropriate utilization of instructional technology.

3. Colleges and universities who are responsible for training prospective teachers for high schools and colleges will have incorporated instruction in the design of courses and in the effective utilization of instructional technology in their curricula.

4. A concerted federal government effort, utilizing the resources of the nation's finest libraries and museums as well as the resources of the nation's campuses, will have been made to design and produce courses of instruction of good quality for presentation using advanced electronic media.

5. At least three cooperative learning-technology centers, combining the instructional technology capabilities of many member institutions within a geographic region, and originating and directing centralized instructional services through information, communications and computing networks, will be in operation.

6. The level of federal support for development and application of instructional technologies should have reached a figure equal to 1 percent of the total national expenditures for higher education.
7. Extramural higher education programs should be available to most Americans through Open University type programs initiated by existing colleges and universities, states, or cooperative learning-technology centers.
8. Legal restraints upon the duplication of educational materials should have been thoroughly reviewed by Congress with special attention given to their impacts on instruction provided by the new technology.
9. Manufacturers of equipment for uses in teaching and learning at colleges and universities will have made a greater effort to adapt their designs so that compatible instructional components can be produced for use on a wide variety of makes and models.
10. Systems for identifying promising instructional materials will have been developed, and procedures for encouraging their development utilization will be operable.
11. New professions for persons engaged in creating and developing instructional materials on the nation's campuses will have emerged.

The commission recommends that the following goals be reached by 1990:
1. Most colleges in the country will have introduced sufficient technologies of all available and appropriate kinds to realize the following benefits: (a) savings of at least 15% of a professor's time per course; (b) provision of alternative modes of instruction for existing courses; and (c) provision of logistical flexibility by allowing students to receive certain amounts of their instruction at times and places that are most convenient for them.
2. Six of the seven proposed cooperative learning-technology centers recommended previously will be in operation.

The commission recommends that the following goals be reached by 2000:
1. All instructional technology identifiable in 1972 will be in general use on college and university campuses.
2. The availability of education through independent study within and without traditional institutions will have become widespread through applications of the expanding technology.

Diversity by Design

The Commission on Non-traditional Study

Jossey-Bass, Publishers, 1973.

The Commission on Non-traditional Study was established in 1971 in response to the rapid developments that had been taking place in higher education. Sponsored by the College Entrance Examination Board and the Educational Testing Service and funded by the Carnegie Foundation, its goals were to examine the whole range of emerging possibilities in non-traditional study, assess the significance of these new trends, and formulate specific recommendations for the future. The commission interpreted its task as research combined with action and shaped both its work and this official final report as a response to that mission. Thus, its two year program of work consisted of four major elements: (1) commission plenary sessions and committee meetings, (2) hearings and conferences with people representing various agencies and institutions related to higher education, (3) commissioned reports and research, and (4) placing the issues relating to non-traditional study before national, regional, and state organizations as well as leaders of individual institutions.

An accurate and comprehensive definition of non-traditional study proved to be one of the commission's most difficult tasks. Few terms were either adequately inclusive or precise. However, most of the members seemed to sense the areas of education around which their mutual interests centered. As Samuel Gould explains in the preface, most of the commissioners agreed that "non-traditional study is more an attitude than a system and thus can never be defined except tangentially. This attitude puts the student first and the institution second, concentrates more on the former's need than the latter's convenience, encourages diversity of individual opportunity rather than uniform prescription, and de-emphasizes time, space, and even course requirements in favor of competence and, where applicable, performance. It has concern for the learner of any age and circumstance, for the degree aspirant as well as the person who finds sufficient reward in enriching life through constant, periodic, or occasional study."

Perhaps the most comprehensive conclusion that the commission was able to arrive at was that the process of educational change must be an evolutionary one. Although there are obvious dichotomies between formal and alternative systems, ultimately one cannot supplant or supersede the other. Non-traditional approaches will augment and enhance traditional philosophies and methods; they will often add new perspectives to educational possibilities; and often they will show that traditional forms have an irreplaceable role to play. Nevertheless, the commission felt that new approaches will increasingly compete with the old for students and funds. Weak institutions, regardless of their approach, will terminate; learning opportunities offered by businesses, proprietary schools and cultural agencies will place a serious drain on the pool of potential students. The formal educational system will have to recognize this competition fairly and dispassionately, for eventually these alternative systems will provide added strength by performing services the older systems are not prepared to undertake and by creating in students a desire for learning which will lead them to the more formal educational system.

Diversity by Design is organized around 57 actionable proposals. Seven of these are of particular importance as they call for major decisions and actions during the next decade. As Samuel Gould has summarized them, these proposals are:

1. Lifetime learning—basic, continuing, and recurrent—has a new appropriateness today and requires a new pattern of support.
2. Colleges and universities must shift emphasis from degree-granting to service to the learner, thus countering what has become a degree-granting obsession.
3. Faculty understandings and commitments must be reoriented and redirected, particularly through in-service development, so that knowledge and use of non-traditional forms and materials will increase.
4. An organized effort must be made to promote intelligent and widespread use of educational technology, with special emphasis on programming for cable television, computers, videotape recorders, and possibilities of satellite broadcasting.
5. New agencies must be created to make possible easy access to information and develop better ways to disseminate it, to perform guidance and counseling services, and to be assessors and repositories of credit for student achievement.
6. New evaluative tools must be developed to match the non-traditional arrangements now evolving, so that accreditation and credentialing will have appropriate measures of quality.
7. Cooperation and collaboration must be encouraged among collegiate, community, and alternate educational entities so that diverse educational programs and structures may come into being.

Chapter Four—Examining Alternatives—is of particular relevance to the focus of this notebook. The commission's recommendations in the chapter are based on the belief that fresh approaches to education are desirable in themselves, because they extend educational opportunity and because they may ultimately feed into the orthodox system. Therefore, the recommendations focus on two intertwining but separable problems: first, the improved use of alternate structures and systems to expand total educational possibilities for students, and second, the widespread use of new technological tools and devices as alternative methods of instruction.

Concerning alternative systems, the commission's recommendations center on making sure that persons involved in directing and teaching within alternative systems should continually examine their policies and practices to be sure that they are providing a sound education; that creative ways of coordinating the work of alternative systems with the academic system of education should be sought; that the resources of communities and regions—particularly of an extended library center—should be inventoried to identify the total educational potential of the area. The commission also recommends that a nationwide council, drawing together representatives of education and the public at large, should be created to build communication and develop creative coordination among the alternative systems of study and the formal academic system and, finally, that government agencies at all levels should coordinate their efforts more efficiently.

The second set of recommendations bears directly on the new technological tools which already have great implications for reaching large numbers of students, offering independent study in a new dimension and effecting financial economies. To the commission, technological development no longer seems to be the principal problem; the existing tools are ample. The problems are rather: the lag between engineering capability and social acceptance; the policies and techniques of management and production, including structural, collaborative, and legal necessities for swift and effective development; the economic unknowns that require research, together with those for start-up costs; the adaptation of teacher education to promote understanding and use of educational technology in appropriate and educationally strengthening ways; the means of effecting economies through the scale and critical mass of operation without creating centralized control.

In examining why there is little acceptance of electronic methods both by educational planners and would-be learners, the commission found resistance rooted in three major fears: that technological methods of instruction would dehumanize the educational process; that technology would turn higher education into a rigid national, homogenized scheme of mass-produced curricula and students; and that technology is actually a substitute to be used when one cannot "do it right." Instead the commission sees technology as opening up the learning experience, offering more individualized, independent study to both traditional students and those who have heretofore been excluded from traditional educational patterns because of location, economic status, age, or family or business responsibilities.

To this end of expanded opportunity, the commission recommends that the potentialities of cable television, videotapes and cassettes, and satellite broadcasting should be carefully scrutinized as an important part of education's future. The commission concludes the chapter by recommending that institutions with common academic interests rather than geographic proximity should organize collaborative arrangements for developing instructional resources appropriate to the capabilities of educational technology. Through joint planning and cooperative action, initiated by participating institutions themselves, one can escape the serious dangers of federal or regional domination and at the same time provide every cooperating institution with a greater range of opportunities and a richer vein of resources than even the largest could achieve on its own.

Other chapters in *Diversity by Design:* Acquiring Perspectives, Broadening Opportunities, Reshaping Institutions and Assessing Accomplishments.

Cable Television
and Higher Education: Two Contrasting Experiences

by Leland Johnson

Rand Corporation Report #R-828-MF, September 1971.

In assessing the promise offered by cable television for serving the needs of educational institutions, the author examines the contrasting experiences of Oregon State University at Corvallis and the University of Oregon at Eugene, each of which employs a channel provided by the cable system serving the local community.

These two institutions use their channels quite differently. Oregon State University (OSU) employs its channel nearly full-time during the day to televise course presentations for students both in and out of the classroom. Video-taped courses are shown twice daily and "recitation" meetings are held on campus each week to allow for student-teacher interaction. These courses, shown exclusively on television are drawn from those having large enrollments. The material is prepared by volunteer professors whose ordinary course loads are reduced in proportion to their televised course loads.

Enrollments in OSU's televised courses have grown impressively over the years and now run to about 8,500 students annually. The annual operating budget is about $70,000 and includes relatively high-quality equipment and services such as the transmission of lessons from the television center to a number of key locations around the campus on a coaxial cable system separate from the Corvallis system that carries the educational channel.

OSU's rationale for employing the cable channel is to save money in faculty salaries and classroom space. Rough calculations suggest that the extent of cost savings depends on (a) the number of students per class in the absence of television, and (b) the cost of faculty time in coursework preparation and presentation. Estimated annual cost savings generated by televised instruction are about $32,000. However, these cost figures do not take into account increased preparation time, differences in the quality of instruction and the total enrollment of the students.

Based on OSU's experience, the author concludes that the key to enhancing the instructional effectiveness of television may lie partially in spending a relatively large amount of money on the preparation of good programming and then sharing the programming with other institutions. Notably, in 1971, an agreement was reached between OSU and the Linn-Benton Community College—which is legally authorized to handle adult or extension courses—to permit joint use of programming on a one-year experimental basis.

During the evening, both the OSU and the community channels are largely vacant. Attractive possibilities for filling the channel with educational programming would arise if the CPB and the PBS could work out satisfactory formal arrangements for serving cable systems, as they now serve non-commercial stations.

In contrast, the University of Oregon uses its channel to supplement and enrich live course presentations in the classroom by providing programming at the request of individual faculty members. The channel also provides a daily message service, an information service as an integral part of the university's registration procedures, and local community programming.

The university is seriously handicapped in filling its cable channel by its dependence on antiquated equipment and by the resulting relatively high maintenance charges. This problem could be alleviated if HEW were permitted by law to fund facilities required for originating programming on cable channels.

Although no definitive answer is given as to why cable use differs at the two institutions, the difference may arise from the fact that Oregon State is an engineering and science institution while the University of Oregon is a liberal arts school. The author hypothesizes that (a) engineering and science courses lend themselves to televised instruction better than do liberal arts courses, and (b) engineering and science faculty and administrators are more amenable to the idea of new technology being employed on the campus.

In conclusion, the author lists four factors which seem especially important in the future use of television in education: first, the ability and willingness of separate institutions to share programming so as to cut costs and improve quality; second, the question of whether differences observed and imputed between liberal art institutions are a general phenomenon; third, the role to be played by the expectation of substantial differences among educational institutions with respect to how they make use of cable channels. As cable moves into major metropolitan areas, the difficulty will lie in deciding how channels are to be allocated among alternative uses within the broad category of education.

Schools and Cable Television

NEA Division of Educational Technology

National Education Association, 1971.

The stated intention of this booklet is to alert the educational community to the opportunities available in the development of cable television and to offer guidelines for the sound development of this new communications system in the public interest. The report opens with a presentation by Harold E. Wigren, (Associate Director, Division of Educational Technology, National Education Association), of five recommendations made by the NEA to the FCC's proposed rule-making committee on CATV systems. These recommendations include:

1. That 20 percent of any old or new CATV system's capacity be reserved for educational, instructional, civic and cultural applications.
2. That the FCC require CATV systems in the top 100 markets to have a minimum capacity of 20 to 24 channels and that the commission compel all systems to stay abreast of the state of the art as regards both channel and

systems capacity.

3. That the commission require two-way capability in all CATV systems.
4. That the proposed public dividend plan—wherein CATV systems in the top 100 markets importing any distant stations would pay 5 percent of their subscription revenues quarterly in the public interest—be adopted and that the public dividend money be reinvested in public cable facilities and programming rather than be allocated to public broadcasting.
5. That local communities should be encouraged to develop experimental public cable corporations dedicated to serving the public interest.

These five recommendations should be applied to both old and new systems so that uniformity of service can be maintained. The NCTA is on record as having a position supportive of the NEA.

The essay by Martha Gable (Editor, *The School Administrator,* American Association of School Administration) stresses the view that whether or not CATV service is provided to schools depends on the initiative of the educational community. When requesting channels, school superintendents and teacher associations should fulfill their obligations by developing proper usage plans including the following considerations: adequate professional leadership, supporting staff, in-service workshops for teachers, adequate facilities and a curriculum planning committee. By properly preparing for cable, full use of its array of services can be made. These services include offering informational programs in several languages, distributing teacher education from local universities, clustering schools so that pupils can exchange live production, and providing high quality individualized instruction at the adult level. The author foresees that cablecasting, rather than broadcasting will be the trend of the 1970s. In the 1980s direct satellite to school transmission will arrive which, when combined with ground cable systems, videotape cassettes/cartridges, facsimile, and eventually lasers, will form a multipurpose informational network. "Hopefully," she concludes, "education will join with the electronics industry in shaping these new developments for the benefit of education."

In the third essay, Frank Norwood (Executive Secretary, Joint Council of Educational Telecommunications) finds upon examining present locally franchised CATV systems that in any given case, the services provided for education are likely to be the result of three factors: (1) the degree of sophistication possessed by those who draw up the ordinance and grant the franchise; (2) the concern of the applicant for educational and community needs; and (3) the interest in CATV shown by the educational community before the franchise is granted.

In order to guarantee the consideration of education's needs by any party, the author recommends that the educator should first determine the status of CATV in his community. If no franchise has been granted, the local educational community itself might become the CATV operator. If the franchise has been granted to a commercial cable operator, the educator can realistically expect that the system will carry either a local or distant ETV station, that the CATV operator will provide free connections to local educational institutions, and that one or more channels will be reserved for educational use.

Greatest mutual benefits may occur when the CATV operator and educators approach the problems of local program origination on the cable and instructional TV for the schools as parts of a whole. Partnerships may be formed for joint purchase, production and use that would eliminate squandering limited resources on separate inadequate efforts.

If the educator finds that his local system was built more than ten years ago and so has become old-fashioned in terms of both franchise and equipment, he will have to explore the possibilities of newer techniques that would create new, essentially private channels for specialized audiences. Here again, the educator must expect to defray part of the costs involved. Mr. Norwood concludes by stressing that regardless of conditions in which he finds his local CATV system, the educator will still and quite properly have to concern himself with matters of program acquisition and production and the proper utilization of program materials once they reach their intended audience. He will still need to budget funds for equipment and personnel and, particularly where the local CATV system is already a going concern, at least a portion of the cost of implementing new educational services over the existing systems. The educator cannot absolve himself from these responsibilities.

In his essay concerning some cost considerations in planning for CATV, D. F. Mikes (Director of Marketing, Educational Information Services, Inc.) suggests that before making substantial investments, school officials should ask several basic questions about ITV in general and CATV in particular to determine the appropriate level for their utilization. These questions cover what is a school's current and projected use of ITV, what kind of production facilities and distribution systems presently exist in schools, whether the school district is capable of supporting CATV-ITV on a per pupil cost basis, whether the system reaches all learning and meeting places in the district, if the reservation of the educational channel is formalized in writing, and whether the cable company will provide free interconnection and use of the channel and will reserve additional channels as new needs arise. The answers to such basic considerations as these will not only determine the most appropriate use of the CATV system to meet particular needs but will also determine the costs involved.

In the final essay of the booklet, Frank Norwood describes some of the unique potentials of cable television for the future. Cable communications offer the opportunity of an abundance of channels, targeted audiences within specific geographical limitations, targeted audiences based on common interests across wide geographical areas, and, still more important, the development of television and other communications as interactive rather than one-way systems. This last characteristic opens up a new world of services on an individual basis.

The Children's Television Workshop—
How and Why It Works

by Herman Land

Nassau Board of Cooperative Educational Services, 1972.

Overview

The distinguishing features of the Children's Television Workshop are:
- A dedication to a justifiable national need.
- A pioneering character and orientation and a "first-time" effort in a recognized social and media "vacuum."
- A highly competent, dedicated management.
- Establishment of a new organization, first as a self-contained unit of National Educational Television (NET), then as an independent nonprofit corporation, to achieve a pioneering goal.
- Sufficient funding to do the full job of preparation, research and production, together with promotion and community involvement, on a professional level.
- Sufficient time to prepare for production.
- A recognition that to compete with commercial television it is necessary to adopt that medium's standards and techniques.
- A recruitment policy which looks upon experienced commercial television talents as the key personnel elements.
- A salary policy that offers as attractions a competitive salary on the lower end of the scale together with the psychic rewards of working in a free creative environment devoted to an important social end.
- An understanding of the complexity of the top management role, which led to the concept of the project director who "pulls it all together" and exercises policy control leaving creative control in the hands of an executive producer.
- A sensitivity to the needs and concerns of creative people, the best of whom resent outside or top management interference as opposed to direction and leadership, and a determination to so organize and operate as to shield them from those pressures.
- A "first among equals" positioning for programming which recognizes its primary role, but which enables the other departments to function equally in the management structure.
- The inclusion of promotion and research as fundamental elements of the Workshop operation from the beginning.
- The recognition that modern audience promotion is a highly specialized function calling for professional expertise, and acceptance of the staffing implications.
- Acceptance of the limitations of white middle-class media for reaching target populations of inner city, Spanish-speaking and rural poor and undertaking a direct community involvement campaign using person-to-person contact as the main element.
- Using research as an integral part of the program development process, testing

segments, and then programs, for attention-holding and educational effectiveness, as well as for overall evaluation of penetration and impact.
- Bringing the professional educator-advisor into an intimate working relationship with the creative and research staffs, so that, from the outset, his expert knowledge informs the process of establishing program curriculum goals.
- An empirical orientation that depends on research feedback in a self-regenerative process of continuous program improvement.
- A concept of the audience as literate where the electronic media are concerned, leading to adoption of contemporary, advanced television production techniques.
- An eclectic approach to technique, which employs film, tape, live action, animation, as indicated, as opposed to reliance on any single technique.
- A nonsequential approach to curriculum based on unpredictable open-circuit viewing patterns, which requires that each program be a self-contained entity from an educational standpoint.
- A determination to become as self-sustaining as possible through the issuance of nonbroadcast materials and international program distribution and a continuing exploration of funding opportunities, coupled with a policy of limiting individual support to nondominant positions in order to preserve operational flexibility and independence.
- A system of cost control, unusual in the nonprofit world, which enables the Workshop to obtain maximum value for its dollars and to maintain overall financial stability.
- An insight into the nature of television program distribution, which led to a major, and largely successful, effort to convince the stations in the noncommercial medium to carry "Sesame Street."

Meeting a National Need

Joan Cooney's proposal for "Sesame Street"—the result of a four month feasibility survey on "Potential Uses of Television in Preschool Education"—responded to what was clearly recognized as a major social need to optimize a child's intellectual stimulation during his most formative preschool years. That this need could not be met by the traditional institutions and resources of the nation's educational system was increasingly obvious. Thus, Ms. Cooney's proposal was especially appropriate as the simple and logical answer to a dilemma that had hitherto resisted solution; its soundness was immediately apparent to anyone who understood the pervaseiveness of the television medium.

Managing a Creative Enterprise

The clarity and precision of the Workshop's purpose—to educate a target population of disadvantaged young children—has functioned as an admirable disciplinary element in organizing the operational energies and talents of the Workshop staff. Its strong appeal to idealism has given the staff a sense of "nationalism" and an environment that is fundamental to the creative process.

The CTW approach to organization begins with the premise that the Workshop is fundamentally a creative institution whose justification is what finally appears on the television screen. Thus its organizational objective is to fashion a creative environment in which the programming team can function freely, not subject to outside pressures from government, industry, political or social groups, or to internal interference from top management itself. This condition is achieved through a structure which presents top management and its supporting administrative and legal staff as the buffers between outside pressure points and the production unit. Creative control rests with the executive producer and his production writing team, while top management retains policy control. This calls for a great degree of mutual trust.

Programming, while it enjoys a "first among equals" status, is freed from direct responsibility for other functions required by the project. There are now seven departments: programming, research, information, finance and administration, community relations, international and special projects, and nonbroadcast materials. The first four were part of the original plan, the others a response to experience.

At the outset, 1968, the Workshop was an autonomous unit within NET, which provided it with legal and administrative services, assistance in distribution, and the corporate "umbrella" needed for grant-receiving purposes. It began its independent existence as a non-profit corporation a year later, in 1969.

Because of the complexity and scale of the proposed venture, Joan Cooney decided early that her role should not be that of executive producer, but *project director*. While the executive producer concentrated on the program production task, the project director would not have a stake in the creative decisions but rather would pull the various elements together: research, professional advisors, station clearances, funding, public information, etc.

Within the programming ranks, one meets with frequent statements that an unusual degree of creative freedom exists. This condition appears to be a reflection of the essentially rational style of those who run the organization and their sense of personal security.

Fusing Education, Research, and Programming

From the beginning of operations, the CTW set out to achieve a working collaboration between the programmer, the educator and the researcher so that all the relevant energies would be funneled into program development from the earliest stages on. Each of the three elements are vital parts of the process of conception, creation and production, and, therefore, the working goals of the project must be simultaneously educationally sound, practical from a television production point of view, and amenable, at least in part, to measurement.

It was decided to put proven commercial television talents in the ultimate decision making positions because, although the Workshop's aim is the direct education of its young target audience, operationally it is a media project, directed and controlled by the television, rather than educational practitioners. In effect the television production team utilizes the knowledge and talents of the educational sector through the instrumentality of the advisor. Instead of the conventional peripheral relationship with programming, the advisor on "Sesame

Street" enjoys an intimate involvement in the program development process. As a member of the operating staff, he is paid for work performed.

One of the Workshop's first projects was to conduct a series of seminars to determine the premises from which precise educational goals could be developed. Approximately 100 educators, researchers, television professionals, writers of children's books, key Workshop creative staff members, and observers from the funding organizations attended these seminars. The meetings were extremely helpful not only because the goals statement that emerged from the session formed the basis of the programmer's final selections of specific goals, but because the creative staff, by participating in all educational planning sessions, had full opportunity to understand both the intent and the goals developed at all stages of curriculum planning.

During the experimental period a major decision was made to emphasize measurable cognitive skills rather than the social or emotional aspects of development. These skills include symbolic representation (letters, numbers), cognitive processes (relational concepts, classification), reasoning, and problem solving. All the major goals are incorporated into each program with specific curriculum assignments spread nonsequentially throughout the series.

The use of field research as an empirical guide in determining what programming is most effective results in production which is, in effect, a self-regenerative process of spiraling improvement. Production is viewed as an open-ended and continuing process rather than as a system with fixed limits.

"Formative" research, directed toward program development, tests both program appeal and teaching effectiveness. "Summative" research, conducted in the "marketplace," tests for penetration—especially in poor urban areas—and overall educational success. The results of this research, as well as the changing conditions of society and their effects on values and attitudes—particularly in relation to humor—are reflected in the continually renewed topical content and treatment of the program.

The research staff never tells the producers that something is not working without offering alternative approaches to an assignment.

Producing the Program

The scope and pioneering aspects of the project allowed no room for amateurism or the perhaps talented but untested skills of a promising producer. Since volume production under commercial conditions was mandatory, the key creative talents have been drawn from commercial network television. There is no advance commitment to program technique. Each program, a self-contained unit, is checked continually for curriculum soundness. This monitoring process is considered helpful rather than restrictive.

Workshop production relations are complex and involve a relatively small staff of producers, writers, and film and tape editors, together with a large number of freelance and subcontract arrangements. This policy permits the Workshop to employ outstanding talents that it could not afford on a full-time basis.

Financial Administration

CTW is run with an efficiency equal to that of any well run commercial institution. In place of the profit motive, it relies on a conscious determination to get $1.25 value for every $1.00 spent. This involves a clear, limited system of budgetary control that all departments must adhere to. Although salaries are marginally competitive, the employee receives part of his reward in the form of "psychic income"—the satisfaction of working for a socially important purpose in an institution where he can enjoy a rare creative freedom.

The CTW principle of budget flexibility calls for an "elastic" approach to financial control which respects creative needs. It starts with the premise that financial administration is not an end in itself but exists to serve the other departments. Implementation of this principle calls for maximum diplomacy and sensitivity to the ways of thinking of those who are not financially oriented. Once the yearly department budget has been worked out, a monthly and daily reporting system goes into effect. By immediately being aware of the budgetary consequences of current and planned activities, the department head can change course if he exceeds his budget or he can follow a desired course by making alterations elsewhere. He still makes the final decision to incur unplanned costs, but he does so aware of the budgetary consequences.

At the end of its first year, the CTW treasury showed $85,000 unspent. The 1971-1972 budget contained $250,000 budgetary reserve for "Sesame Street" and $100,000 reserve for "The Electric Company."

The Importance of Promotion

The information-promotion function was built into the CTW as a basic structural element. It is fully professional in the staff and operation. Through an arrangement with a public relations firm, the Workshop has its in-house executive and team on permanent placement plus an outside task force for specific assignment.

As the first educational televison undertaking to mount a "big-league" promotional publicity campaign, CTW used little paid advertising, depending instead on the public relations art. The many-sided initial campaign involved press releases, brochures, newspaper and magazine stories and interviews, television and radio announcements, appearances before public and industry groups, trade promotion devices, an innovative electronic press conference and a unique preview of the series on NBC. The cooperation of commercial networks was unparalleled.

Reaching the Disadvantaged

The ultimate target audience was the disadvantaged child of the inner city ghetto and the remote rural area. The CTW had to overcome the limitations of the white middle-class media, the overall white, cultural-elite orientation of public television, the low audience levels associated with that medium, and the prevalence of UHF in the non-commercial spectrum, all of which made contact with target populations difficult to achieve.

Therefore, a large-scale community involvement campaign was undertaken to inform the black, Spanish-speaking and poor rural white populations that "Sesame Street" was available to them. It was based on personal contact with parental groups and organizations, the setting up of viewing centers, the distribution of handbills, and the use of displays at shopping centers. Since then the field service staff has moved on to a continuing extensive utilization campaign that involves parents to help them help their children to benefit from the instructional content of the program.

Getting the Program on the Air

In order to obtain "station clearances," Joan Cooney and her executive assistant, Robert Davidson, visited the top 25 markets to meet with school representatives and station managers. The obstacle was the instructional school service programming that fills the daily schedule of so many non-commercial stations. The effort was successful and "Sesame Street" achieved wide distribution with morning time in stations covering about 60 percent of the population

Multiple Funding Sources

Out of CTW's $7.2 million budget for the first two years, 55 percent went to production, 16.8 percent went to research, 7 percent went to distribution, 8.4 percent went to promotion, and 9.8 percent went to administration costs. The U.S. Office of Education contributed 50 percent of the first year's budget with matching amounts generated through grants from the U.S. Office of Economic Opportunity, the National Institute for Child Health and Human Development, the National Foundation on the Arts and Humanities, the John and Mary Markle Foundation and the Corporation for Public Broadcasting.

CTW management is convinced that multiple sources of funding are important for operational flexibility and sustained support. Given a desired maximum level of 33-1/3 percent government involvement, remaining long-range funding sources may include: (1) sale of program distribution rights to the Corporation for Public Broadcasting; (2) grants by industry; (3) sales of non-broadcast materials; (4) sales of programs and program rights to other countries; (5) proceeds from an endowment fund, should one be established.

The Workshop in Perspective

"Given the central problem of survival, which will plague all future organizations that draw their inspriation from its achievement, the primary national requirement appears evident. The starting point of any significant national effort to enlarge upon the accomplishments of the Children's Television Workshop is a determination to build that institution into a secure and permanent feature of the American educational scene. Only when that has been done will the model be complete."—Land Report, p. 211

The Open University

by John Scupham

The International Broadcast Institute of England, 1972.

I. *Origins, History and Constitution*

The Open University of England received its charter in 1969 and started its teaching operations in January 1971. As it enters its third year, the University already has become an established national institution with a smoothly functioning operational center, a national network of vigorous local activities, and 40,000 enthusiastic students. Termed by this report's author as "the most ambitious attempt yet made to enlist the broadcasting media in the service of higher education," it was created in partial response to the Robbins Report on Higher Education of 1963, which called for the provision of enough new places by 1980 to raise from 8 percent to 17 percent the proportion of the population profiting from advanced studies.

Although the planners of the Open University studied many examples of pioneer broadcast correspondence courses in countries such as Japan, France, Australia, and America, their venture differs from all others in that it is not an extension of an existing university, but rather is an autonomous, independent, degree-giving institution enjoying a full measure of academic freedom and a machinery of government similar to other recent established universities. Its governing body is a Council, with members nominated by the government, the Committee of Vice-Chancellors and Principals of existing universities, local education authorities, the BBC, and the University's own Senate. The Senate, representing the staff, exercises control over the curriculum and methods of teaching. A small Academic Advisory Committee of distinguished scholars drawn from other universities has the duty of keeping an independent eye on course content and the conduct of examinations.

The government's role in the creation of this controversial institution was decisive. In 1964, with the leadership of Harold Wilson, the Labour Party enacted plans for a "University of the Air" by gathering a small Advisory Committee under the chairmanship of Lady Jenny Lee. Despite conservative university attitudes, resentment at this new diversion of educational resources, and a uniformly hostile press, this Committee issued an official White Paper which firmly upheld the original intention that this new institution was to be truly a university.

The Advisory Committee was succeeded by a Planning Committee of distinguished educators who worked out a comprehensive plan for an "Open University," drafted the Charter and Statutes, won over higher education on a national level, and established representative liaison committees that linked the University with local education authorities, the teaching profession, the libraries, and the educational branches of the armed forces. The Report of the Planning Committee was published early in 1969. The Committee remained in being to recruit the nucleus of the University staff until July, when it handed over its powers to the Council and Senate as constituted by the University Charter.

II. *Staff Recruitment and Student Enrollment*

The policy governing staff recruitment follows directly from the emphasis on full university status. Senior posts are filled by men and women of the highest academic distinction, who are assured that they will have the same time and facilities for research and writing that they would enjoy at any other university.

The Planning Committee envisioned its student body as composed of men and women with jobs and family responsibilities who had been unable to complete a degree either because they were born too early to profit from an increasing range of opportunities for higher education; because they had been distracted by the pressure of work, domestic circumstances, or the lack of some preliminary qualification; or because they simply wanted to bring their knowledge up to date, frequently for vocational reasons. Although admissions are largely on a "first-come, first-served" basis, attempts were made to spread the student body out both in geographical and subject matter areas; preference was given to members of less privileged occupational groups. A regionally based counselling service was provided to help potential students assess their ability to work at the required level, to advise them on the choice of courses, and if necessary, to guide them toward preparatory courses at a lower level. Seventy percent of the applicants were male. percent between the ages of 25-34.

III. *Course Structure and Curriculum*

The University utilizes the one-year course as a basic credit unit, but achieves greater flexibility through ½-credit courses at more advanced levels. These one-year courses are grouped in six main "lines" of study—arts, educational studies, mathematics, science, social sciences, and technology—and are of four levels. For each line there is an introductory "foundation course"; only after a student successfully has completed a credit in at least one foundation course may he choose to specialize, and he may continue to draw on courses from other faculties if he wishes. The B.A. degree is awarded to a student who obtains six credits, two in foundation courses and four in second or subsequent levels. Courses need not be taken in successive years and no more than two credit courses may be taken in the same year. A degree of some other university, a professional qualification of equivalent standing, a teacher training certificate, or a diploma in technology may entitle him to a maximum of three credit exemptions, thus allowing him to concentrate his energies on a narrower field and substantially shorten his path to a degree.

All of the foundation courses and those second level courses for which there is most demand are to be offered every year, the others in appropriate rotation, and each course will be offered four times before it is remade.

IV. *Preparation of Courses*

In accordance with the principle that academic content and the ways in which it is taught must be thought of as a single operation by the same group of people, "course teams" are entrusted with the total responsibility for a single year of half-year course. Each team is composed of teachers whose special province is involved, experts from the outside, representatives of those departments of the University primarily concerned with learning strategies, with teaching methods, and with media production, and the radio and television producers who will be responsible for the broadcast component of the course. An editor in each team is responsible for the coordination of its work.

A "systems approach" is taken to teaching—educational objectives are specified; the students' task is broken down into its component parts; learning processes are identified; the appropriateness of the teaching methods available in relation to each stage is considered; methods are combined so that they will make up an integrated whole; and finally, feedback, validation, and assessment procedures are established.

V. *Teaching Methods—Correspondence Tuition*

It has been recognized from the first that broadcasting could not possibly carry the main expository burden of the Open University for sheer lack of available airtime. The only method of instruction (1) capable of indefinite extension as new needs arise and (2) capable of being made available everywhere is correspondence. Further, this is a method that allows for two-way traffic of ideas, but at an individual's own time and pace. An Open University student receives at regular intervals a package of correspondence materials and, where relevant, slides, films, records, or science kits for home experiments. The written material includes references to other reading, home self-test questions, and a guide to the relevant television and radio programs. The student is given assignments at regular intervals to be marked by his tutor or by a computer.

Broadcasting

The Planning Committee made the assumption that every one-year course provided should be able to make use of one television and one radio program in each week of the academic year. Thus, broadcasting is an integral part of course work. Employing a full range of resources in a wide variety of ways, it is used to make the initial presentation of a series of topics with the maximum impact, leaving the task of development and consolidation to the correspondence teaching. Individual programs illustrate points of special difficulty in the light of student feedback; they convey aesthetic experience in ways that transcend the functions of the more utilitarian package; they give students the feeling that they are members of a corporate body and are in contact with the teaching staff; and they expose the general public to the possibilities of higher education.

Through its Institute of Educational Technology, the University carries out research to build up a reliable body of knowledge about the dynamics of broadcast program effectiveness. For the Open University, broadcasting is simply one element to be considered in its functional relationship with other elements of a course. It remains an open question whether broadcast transmission is the best way of distributing such audio-visual material as proves to be required.

Study Centers

Since broadcasts are presently important, arrangements have to be made to ensure that they are universally accessible. Thus, students may regularly attend one of the 284 Study Centers which have been established throughout the United Kingdom. All of them are equipped for the direct reception and for the tape-recording of both radio and TV media. The Centers in areas of poor reception hold libraries of all the television programs transmitted and other Centers may borrow copies from the regional headquarters.

However, the Study Centers are more than broadcast receiving centers. Organized in twelve regions, they provide the basis for personal tutorial services to students and the framework for their corporate life as undergraduates. A locally based counselor is available at each of the Study Centers on specific evenings of every week and students may ask for a personal interview every fortnight. No student is obliged to use the Centers. Nevertheless, experience suggests that three-fourths of the registered students appreciate the opportunities that the Centers provide—including a strong corporate sense and a lively social life.

One element of face-to-face teaching is obligatory. Each foundation course includes a summer session which lasts a week and provides an intensive period of full-time study during which students enjoy greater personal contact with their professors and their peers.

VI. The Broadcasting Operation

Broadcasting arrangements are the subject of a five-year agreement and contract with the BBC, which is responsible for supplying both staff and studios. The main stumbling block in negotiating these arrangements proved to be the question of air-time. The BBC did not feel able to offer peak evening time for minority purposes. Ultimately, it was agreed that a maximum of thirty hours of television time on its second channel, BBC 2, and thirty hours of radio time would be devoted to the originations and repeats of the University's programs. Originations are spaced throughout the week in the early evening and repeats are placed in a block on Sunday mornings.

The second source of difficulty in the negotiations with the BBC was the formulation of a proper constitutional relationship between two independent bodies, each of them concerned to establish and define its own sphere of action. The University has the ultimate responsibility for every aspect of its actions, but the Corporation has reserved the right of action in the practical conduct of the broadcast operation, and its educational department was anxious to ensure that it would be able to make a creative contribution to the achievement of the University's academic standards. Accordingly, while remaining an integral part of the BCC operationally, its educational department has become a major part of the University. BBC producers participate on the course teams and are represented formally on both the Senate and the Council.

Since programming requires a full range of resources and programming techniques, the BBC has had to lease separate premises and equip them as the home of a largely self-contained operation devoted solely to Open University purposes. The operation is sustained by a production staff of 100. Most of the senior producers have been specifically recruited and trained for Open University operations and recruited furthermore as subject specialists capable of playing a full part in the course teams.

Broadcast services are charged at their cost price.

VII. *Costs and Cost-Effectiveness*

The University expects to have spent $5 million on its buildings and equipment by the end of 1973. Since the cost of course planning and development depends on the number of academic staff involved rather than the number of students, cost per student will diminish sharply with increasing numbers. In addition, many construction and production costs can be considered initial rather than continuing. The largest portion of money comes from a direct government grant. Local education authorities meet the expenses of the summer school for students in their own areas.

It is natural that questions of cost-effectiveness should be raised and the University has embarked on a joint study with the London School of Economics of the comparative cost-effectiveness of all forms of higher education. Findings, of course, will influence future developments.

The main task before the University in the years immediately ahead is that of implementing its plans for courses leading to a first degree, validating and improving its methods, and assessing the strength of effective demand in the various fields of study. Future potential projects include post-graduate and "post-experience" courses, and the admission of qualified school dropouts. Pilot experiments along these lines are being considered with more conventional institutions of higher education.

The Vice-Chancellor has formulated his own provisional view of the necessary conditions for the continued success of the Open University. They include a large pool of persons who are capable of higher education but were denied it, a distribution network that is adequate, and an adequate pool of qualified part-time teachers. But even where these conditions do not exist, the work of the University may well prove to have far-reaching significance. Its operations are resulting in the production of new teaching materials in printed and recorded form which constitute complete and integrated courses. It is the belief of the University that the use of its methods and materials in existing universities and colleges may well enable them to launch out in new directions and extend the range of subjects that they offer, to provide services to an increased number of students, and to achieve a real economy of academic manpower.

For a further cost analysis of the Open University, see: *The Economics of the Open University* by Leslie Wagner, Higher Education, Elsevier Publishing Co., Amsterdam, 1972.

In order to give some broad indication of the cost differences between the Open University and conventional universities, this paper makes four comparisons between the two types of institutions in teaching students and producing graduates. These are: the average recurrent cost per equivalent undergraduate, in which the Open University cost is little more than a quarter of conventional universities; the capital cost per student place, where the Open University figure is about 6 percent of the conventional figure; the average recurrent cost per graudate, which indicates that the cost at the two types of institutions would be equalized if the Open University had a drop-out rate of 85 percent; and the resource cost per equivalent undergraduate, where the Open University costs are about a sixth of conventional costs.

These differences seem to be due in part to the fact that: (1) the Open University has a high ratio of fixed to variable costs in which many recurrent expenditures are not directly linked to the number of students participating, *i.e.,* an increase in students does not mean more faculty or facilities; (2) students are not physically on campus and so cultural, recreational, library and miscellaneous facilities do not have to be provided; (3) production techniques—correspondence media, radio and televison—produce economies of scale.

The paper makes the tentative suggestion that it is not the part-time nature of the students which is important, but the method of teaching which gives the Open University its advantage. The paper suggests that in a period of increasing pressure on the resources of higher education, the application of the Open University teaching methods to conventional universities should be studied.

Glossary

cablecasting Televised programming distributed directly through a cable system, as distinguished from re-transmitted broadcast signals. Includes the cable operator's own programs, as well as programs on public- and educational-access and on leased channels.

Cable Television Information Center A non-profit center in Washington, D.C. that provides assistance and information to local government authorities engaged in granting cable television franchises.

CATV *Community Antenna Television,* an older term referring to systems providing primarily improved television signal reception. Now generally supplanted by the term *cable television* or *cable.*

CLEP *College Level Examination Program,* a national examination, administered by the Educational Testing Service, which is used for granting college-level credit for work done outside of college.

courseware A combination of textbooks, other written instructional materials, and the various audio-visual instructional materials, such as film, audio and video tape, slides, computer tapes, etc. See also *hardware* and *software.*

CPB — The *Corporation for Public Broadcasting,* established by Congress in 1967 to promote and finance development of non-commercial radio and television in the United States. CPB receives funds from both government and private sources.

educational access channel — One of three cable channels required by the 1972 FCC ruling for all new cable television systems in the 100 largest U.S. television markets. The channel, which is to be available free for a trial period of five years, is reserved solely for use by local "educational authorities," although administrative responsibility for the channel remains with the cable operator.

ETV — *Educational Television,* an older term for the non-commercial system now referred to as *public television.*

external degree — A degree program in higher education in which attendance of on-campus classes is not required.

extramural education — The offering of educational courses or programs off campus through the use of independent study, correspondence, remote learning centers, the media, or a combination of these. Also referred to as *open learning.*

FCC — The *Federal Communications Commission,* the U.S. agency responsible for the regulation of cable as well as broadcast television and other forms of telecommunications.

franchise — The contractual agreement by which a local government grants the right and sets the conditions for a company to operate a cable system within a particular jurisdiction.

formative research — The process developed by Children's Television Workshop, by which the testing of program materials for effectiveness contributes to the final design of those programs.

FTE — *Full-time equivalency,* the unit for measuring overall attendance in public institutions of higher education. (Two students attending half-time equal one "FTE".) The amount of state funds to colleges is usually based on the total number of FTE's.

hardware
Refers to the machinery—projectors, television equipment, computers, teaching machines—used in audio-visual institution. See also *courseware* and *software.*

head end
In a cable system, the place at which all signals are electronically processed for distribution through the cable. Generally located at the system's antenna site.

ITV
Instructional television, the use of television teaching as a component of the in-school curriculum.

leased channel
A cable channel leased by the system operator to another party. The 1972 FCC cable rules require that cable channels be available for lease at non-discriminatory rates.

local origination
Programs supplied over cable by the operator himself—usually on a single channel reserved for that use.

major markets
The 100 areas with the largest number of television viewers, as defined by the FCC. The 1972 FCC cable rules specify different requirements for the top 50 markets, markets 51-100, and markets below the top 100.

module
A package of teaching materials forming a single, discrete component of a larger educational program or an entire course. It may be a self-contained lesson or part of a lesson.

MSO
Multiple System Operator, a company which owns more than one cable system.

National Center for Educational Technology
A new agency of the United States Office of Education which is responsible for promoting innovations in the uses of telecommunications and other technologies for education.

open learning
See *extramural education.*

Open University
The institution established in England to provide higher education by means of television and radio broadcasts, correspondence, and study centers. Several American universities are now experimenting with the use of course materials developed by the Open University.

pay-cable
A system for providing special programming over cable

for a fee in addition to the basic monthly cable subscription. Usually involves the use of a home terminal to permit viewing of signal which is scrambled or transmitted on a non-standard channel.

PBS

The *Public Broadcasting Service,* which has been responsible for the national programming of public television, as well as operating the national public television interconnection (or network) system.

penetration

The ratio of homes subscribing to cable to the number of homes passed by a cable system.

proprietary school

A privately owned, profit-making educational institution.

public-access channel

A channel required by the 1972 FCC rules for new major market systems, to be available free for programming by the general public on a first-come, first-served basis. Although required to administer the channel, the cable operator is not allowed to censor public-access programming in any way.

public television

See *ETV, CPB* and *PBS.*

two-way system or capacity

A cable system which can carry signals from subscriber homes to the system head end, as well as from head end to subscriber. The 1972 FCC rules require that new systems in the major markets be built with two-way capacity, though actual two-way service is not required. Only a few experimental two-way systems are currently in operation.

software

Generic term used, particularly in education, for any programs developed for a computer. See also *courseware* and *hardware.*

S-U-N

The acronym for the *State University of Nebraska,* a non-campus, media-based institution being developed by the University of Nebraska at Lincoln to provide college-level courses to homes.

UHF

Ultra-high frequency, referring to TV channels 14-83. Most public television stations are on the UHF band, although reception of UHF signals is often more difficult than VHF signals. Cable television can help equalize UHF and VHF reception.

VHF   *Very high frequency,* referring to television channels 2-13.

Annotated
Bibliography

Continuing Education and Non-Traditional Study

American Council on Education. "Higher Education and the Adult Student."
A.C.E. Special Report. Washington, D.C., October 25, 1972.

Commission on Non-Traditional Study. *Diversity by Design.* San Francisco:
Jossey-Bass, 1973.

See Abstracts, pp. 149-151.

Dennis, Lawrence E. "The Other End of Sesame Street," in G. Kerry Smith, ed.,
New Teaching–New Learning. San Francisco: Jossey-Bass, 1971, pp. 57-64.

A call for an "Open University of North America" in which television
would be the principle teaching medium supplemented by radio, correspondence materials, films, tapes, etc.

Diridon Research Corporation. *Survey of Attitudes toward Higher and Continuing Education in Northeastern California* (for California Coordinating
Council on Higher Education). Sacramento, April 15, 1972.

Gould, Samuel, and Cross, K.P. *Explorations in Non-Traditional Study.* San
Francisco: Jossey-Bass, 1972. Compiled with the assistance of the ERIC
Clearinghouse on Media and Technology, Stanford University.

Johnstone, John W.C., and Rivera, Ramon J. *Volunteers for Learning: A Study of the Educational Pursuits of American Adults.* Chicago: Aldine Publishing Co., 1965, pp. 1-2.

The largest single survey to date of adult interest and participation in education.

Marien, Michael. "Space-free/Time-free Higher Learning: New Programs, New Institutions and New Questions." *Notes on the Future of Education.* Winter 1972, pp. 6-11.

An exploration of alternative methods of higher education that are easily applicable to other than post-secondary institutions.

Moses, Stanley. *The Learning Force: A More Comprehensive Framework for Educational Policy.* Syracuse University, 1971.

A statistical study of the number of adults engaged in educational pursuits.

Nelson, Fred. "The Open University in the United States." *College Board Review.* Fall 1972, pp. 11-14.

A report on four experiments using Open University material in the United States.

Newman, Frank, *et al. Report on Higher Education.* Washington, D.C.: Government Printing Office, 1971.

A critique of current developments of higher education in the United States. Calls for more options, more attention to the needs of older students.

Perspectives of Adult Education in the United States and a Projection for the Future. Report for the Third International UNESCO Conference on Adult Education, Tokyo, Japan, July 25-August 7, 1972. Washington, D.C.: Department of H.E.W., 1972.

An assessment of adult education in terms of the characteristics of the learner, his effects on the economy, organizational and administrative requirements, and future directions.

Valley, John R. *Increasing the Options—Recent Developments in College and University Degree Programs.* Educational Testing Service, September 1972.

Zigerell, James J. "Universities without Walls and No Illusions." *Educational Television.* October 1971, pp. 17-18.

A look at the less traditional forms of higher education, including instructional television, evening divisions and extensions. Notes the surge in interest in college-of-the-air and comments on some of the possible pitfalls in light of some of the author's 15 years experience with Chicago's TV College.

Television-Supported Education—General Studies

Alter, Henry C. *Of Messages and Media: Teaching and Learning by Public Tele-vision—Notes and Essays on Education for Adults.* Brookline, Mass.: Center for the Study of Liberal Education for Adults, 197?.

An analysis and interpretation of the special methods and style of public television as an educational medium, with a view toward more effective cooperation between PTV and the educational world.

Breitenfeld, Frederick. "Instructional Television: The State of the Art," in Sidney G. Tickton, ed., *To Improve Learning: An Evaluation of Instructional Technology,* Vol. I. New York: Bowker, 1970, pp. 137-160.

A practical description of instructional television activity from the technical, educational and political standpoints. Indicates the strengths and opera-tional limitations of alternative types of systems. Also provides a broad list of on-going applications of instructional TV.

Carnegie Commission on Higher Education. *The Fourth Revolution—Instruction-al Technology in Higher Education.* New York: McGraw-Hill, June 1972.

See Abstracts, pp. 143-148.

Chu, Goodwin C., and Schramm, Wilbur. *Learning from Television: What the Research Says.* Washington, D.C.: National Association of Educational Broadcasters, 1967.

See Abstracts, pp. 133-137.

Dubin, Robert, and Hedley, Alan. *The Medium May Be Related to the Message.* University of Oregon: Center for the Advanced Study of Educational Administration, 1969.

See Abstracts, pp. 137-138.

Hearings on Educational Technology, May 5, 1971, and September 13, 1972. Washington, D.C.: U.S. House Select Subcommittee on Education.

Hearings on HR 1916, a bill for educational technology for pre-school, elementary and secondary education. Contains *The Fourth Revolution* statements on video cassettes, and a report on a 1969 conference on a "Reappraisal of the Educational Technology Industry."

Hudson, Robert B. *The Future of Educational Television*. Washington, D.C.:
    Academy for Educational Development, Inc., 1968.

International Council for Educational Development. *Instructional Broadcasting:
    A Design for the Future* (the "Perkins Report"). Corporation of Public
    Broadcasting, January 15, 1971.

    A report stressing that the successful development of instructional TV re-
    quires a fresh look at the whole educational system. Calls for programs for
    high school and college-level equivalency and for vocational training to
    equal $16 million and recommends that the Corporation for Public Broadcast-
    ing take a lead in initiating these programs.

Jones, Ken. "Community Television." *Adult Education* (Great Britain). Vol. 37,
    March 1965, pp. 313-326.

Niemi, John A., ed. *Mass Media and Adult Education*. Englewood Cliffs, N.J.:
    Educational Technology Publications, 1971.

    A collection of essays written by American, British and Canadian educators
    presenting several ideas for using mass media more effectively in adult
    education.

Norwood, Frank. *Educational Technology and Non-Traditional Study*. Commis-
    sion on Non-Traditional Study, n.d.

    An argument for the natural alliance between technology and non-tradi-
    tional study. Calls for "discipline-based" production centers.

Tickton, Sidney G., ed. *To Improve Learning: An Evaluation of Instructional
    Technology* (2 vol.). New York: Bowker, 1970.

Walton, Wesley W. *New Paths for Adult Learning—Systems for the Delivery of
    Non-Traditional Studies*. Educational Testing Service, October 20, 1972.

    A review of cassettes, CATV and the need for technological resource curri-
    culum and research service centers.

Television-Supported Education—Specific Programs

Bretz, Rudy. *Three Models for Home-based Instructional Systems Using Tele-
    vision*. Santa Monica: Rand Report R-1089-USOEMF, October
    1972.

    See Abstracts, pp. 138-142.

Carlisle, Robert D.B. *The Adult Learning Program Service* (ALPS) *Report for May 1-November 1, 1972.* Corporation for Public Broadcasting, October 13, 1972.

>A description of the ALPS program, which aimed to reach 8.5 million adults between 25 and 45 who had not completed high school and teach them reading and math skills they could use at home and on the job. This project was cancelled by the Corporation for Public Broadcasting in 1972.

Cooney, Stuart. *A Three-Year Plan.* The Northern California Regional Instructional Television Consortium, California State University at Sonoma, December 15, 1972.

>A proposal for the development of a media-based external educational system involving a consortium of colleges and universities in Northern California.

Fagan, Brian M. "The Education of a Professor: The Sequel." *Educational Television.* January 1971, pp. 13-16.

>A description of the evolution of a multi-media anthropology course at the University of California at Santa Barbara. Course includes television as only one of a whole battery of educational media.

Kobin, William. *A Proposal for Twenty-six One-Hour Television Programs on Health.* Children's Television Workshop, Future Works Division, November 1972.

Land, Herman W. *Children's Television Workshop—How and Why It Works.* Nassau Board of Cooperative Educational Services, 1972.

>See Abstracts, pp. 156-161.

Lesser, Gerald S. "Learning, Teaching and Television Production for Children: The Experience of Sesame Street." *Harvard Educational Review.* May 1972, pp. 232-271.

>A discussion of how educational goals are translated into actual television programming. Reflections on the experience of researchers and television producers working together to develop television for children on the basis of knowledge about how children learn.

Meierhenry, Wesley C. "Sun is Rising." *Audio-Visual Instruction.* October 1972, pp. 44-45,47.

Nader, Shafeek. "Cable TV and the Community College." *Community and Junior College Journal.* November 1972 (special issue).

Issue also contains articles on the Vincennes University educational use of
its cable system, on the Coast Community Colleges and the Miami-Dade
Junior College innovative ETV programming, and on decision factors involved in forming a consortium for educational television.

WGBH Educational Foundation. "The ITV Humanities Project: A History of Five
Experimental Programs for Instructional Television." Boston, 1968.

A report on the problems related to producing five ITV programs intended
to show an innovative, interdisciplinary approach to the teaching of humanities at the high school level. Sponsored by the National Endowment
for the Humanities.

Cable and Education

Cablevision for Continuing Education and Community Programs. Conference presentations, Saskatchewan Association for Lifelong Learning, Regina, November 28-29, 1972.

Emphasis on the value of cable as a tool for enhancing interaction within
the community.

Carpenter, Polly. *Cable Television: A Guide for Education Planners.* Santa Monica:
Rand Report R-1144-NSF, May 1973.

Carpenter, Polly. *Cable Television: Uses in Education.* Santa Monica: Rand Report
R-1143-NSF, May 1973.

These two volumes are part of a series of 12 reports prepared by Rand,
under the direction of Walter Baer, for the National Science Foundation.
The report on "Uses in Education" surveys current educational television
programs, describes the ways in which cable could benefit education, and
discusses "the educator's stake in the cable TV franchise." The companion
"Guide for Education Planners" is a more technical report on planning,
developing, and operating an educational project using cable.

"Classroom in the Home via Cable." *Broadcast Management/Engineering.* October
1971.

"College Comes to New York Cable Subscribers." *NCTA Bulletin.* September 28,
1971, p. 2.

Council for Cultural Cooperation. *Second Seminar on Direct Teaching by Television.* Council of Europe, Strasbourg, 1969.

Proceedings from a conference held to promote coordination between educational authorities and radio and television experts in their assessment of adult educational needs and their evaluation of the results of experimental educational television programming.

Dordick, H.S. *Business Plan Edu-cable: Educational Training and Leisure-Time Services via a Leased CATV Channel.* U.S. Office of Telecommunications Policy, n.d.

See Part II, pp. 119-124.

Dunn, D.A. "Cable Television Delivery of Educational Services." IEEE Eascon Conference, Washington, D.C., October 6-8, 1971.

An examination and typical costs of four types of instructional TV systems: (1) conventional instructional TV, (2) interactive instructional TV using subscriber response capability, (3) interactive instructional TV with subscriber voice feedback, (4) interactive individualized instruction and library-like services using single-frame local storage technology.

Fischer, Floyd B., and Nead, Benjamin M. "The Potential of Cable Television for Adult Education." *NUEA Spectator.* March 1972.

Hanley, Anne. *Cable Television and Education—A Report from the Field.* Washington, D.C.: The National Cable Television Association, March 1973.

A status report appraising some of the exploratory steps that have been taken to utilize cable television in education, including increased school-community contact and do-it-yourself television and programming for the "sandbox," the "ivory tower" and the library. Appendices contain the NCTA Educational Telecommunications Policy statement, FCC rules governing access channels, and a list of colleges and universities which use cable for educational programs.

Harley, William G. "The Common Concerns of Educational Television and CATV," *Cablecasting and Educational Television.* 1968, pp. 20-21.

Johnson, Leland L. *Cable Television and Higher Education: Two Contrasting Experiences.* Rand Report R-828-MF, September 1971.

See Abstracts, pp. 152-153.

Joint Council on Educational Telecommunications. "Negotiating for Educational Channels on CATV—a JCET Memo." Washington, D.C.

Kenney, Brigitte L., and Norwood, Frank W. "CATV: Visual Library Service." *American Libraries.* July/August 1971, pp. 723-726.

Description of the general types of services which CATV might make available to public libraries. Also, an outline of the steps to be taken in gaining access to channel capacity.

Lastinger, R. Leroy. "How to Get Along with a CATV System." *Educational Television.* July 1971, pp. 10-11.

A brief explanation of the agreements reached between the ETV and CATV systems in Florida, preventing an overlap of educational programming.

Livingston, Harold. "Between College and Community: CATV Provides the Perfect Link." *TV Communications.* March 1970.

Description of the successful partnership between Oregon State University and the local cable system, written by the head of the university's audio-visual center.

Macy, John. *Public Broadcasting and CATV.* Sloan Commission, n.d.

Calls for public television stations to become "community centers for education and public service."

Marchese, Lamar. "Cable TV—And Adult Education." *Adult Leadership.* March 19, 1971, pp. 299-300, 315-316.

A brief introductory article calling for increased cooperation between adult education and CATV at a national level through such measures as a conference and the formation of a national cable television network.

Molenda, Michael H. "CATV and Access to Knowledge," in Bruce Heitler and Kas Kalba, eds. *The Cable Fable,* special issue of the *Yale Review of Law and Social Action.* Vol. 2, Spring 1972, pp. 243-251.

A consideration of how CATV could serve as a distribution technology for ETV. Includes discussion of remote retrieval of programming, CAI, and some of the regulatory implications of an educationally oriented system.

Nathanson, Marc B. "CATV: A Better Way to Educate." *Adult Leadership.* April 1972, pp. 352 ff.

A suggestion that cable television has much to offer adult education as a supplement to today's growing educational needs.

National Education Association. *Schools and Cable Television.* Washington, D.C.,

See Abstracts, pp. 153-155.

Parker, Edwin. *Stanford Cable Television Committee to Federal Communications Commission.* Cable Television Inquiry, Docket #18397A, December 4, 1970.

A description of a private university's interest in cable television regulations and the results they hope those regulations will accomplish.

Silverstone, David M. "The Role of Cable TV in Continuing Education." *Journal of Continuing Education and Training.* May 1972, pp. 289-295.

Singer, Benjamin D. *Cablecast.* Ottawa: Canadian Department of Communications, Report S-DEC-1, n.d.

A study of the viewing patterns of locally originated community cablecasting in Ontario. Describes the efforts needed to reach an audience effectively via cable.

Smith, Ralph Lee. "Ownership Policy and the Cable Industry." *Yale Review of Law and Social Action.* Spring 1972, pp. 266-67.

Stevens, Robert R. "The Vincennes Project: A Study in ETV-CATV Relationships." *Educational Television.* July 1971, pp. 12-14.

A report on Vincennes University's ETV station, which is operated on the profits derived from the two local CATV systems owned by the university.

Strimel, George. "CATV: A Report from the Front Lines." *Educational and Industrial Television.* May 1972.

A description of the author's difficulties in getting educational broadcast programming onto the local cable system and of the various methods he used to increase coverage of his programs.

Surpin, Shelley. "The Fluid University, 1996." *College and University Business.* September 1971, pp. 8-10.

A look at the university of the future, the structure of which is shaped by the emerging communications technologies. Video cassettes and CATV are seen as the major revolutionizing forces.

Vento, Charles J. "Making the Most of CATV." *Educational Television.* July 1971, pp. 9-10.

A brief exploration of the specific ways cable can be used to fill specific needs both in and out of schools. Emphasizes the distinction between reservation of educational channels and achievement of *access* to channel capacity.

Wilhelms, Fred T. "Cable TV—Protecting Its Future in Education." *Interpretations: An Occasional Paper.* Washington, D.C.: Association for Supervision and Curriculum Development, National Education Association, November 1971.

Related Educational Technologies

Education Products Information Exchange. "Computer-Assisted Instruction." *Educational Product Report No. 45.* New York, 1972.

A balanced yet positive overview of several operational computer systems. Specifications of types of computer-based services are provided as well as cost information.

Education Products Information Exchange. "Instructional Television Fixed Service." *Educational Product Report No. 31.* New York, 1971, pp. 12-15, 27-58.

A description of the FCC's special 2,500 MGZ educational-channels allocation known as ITFS. Includes an outline of the basic technology and discussion of cooperative approaches to its utilization and a list of existing ITFS users and the characteristics of their systems.

Mitre Corporation. *Toward a Market Success for CAI—An Overview of TICCIT.* June 1972.

A full presentation of Mitre's TICCIT (Time-shared, Interactive Computer-Controlled Information Television), a pilot project aimed at catalyzing the mass dissemination of CAI and achieving a major market success for this method of instruction within five years.

Morgan, R.P., Singh, J.P., Anderson, B.D., and Greenberg, E. "Satellites for U.S. Education: Needs, Opportunities and Systems." St. Louis, Mo.: Washington University, April 1972.

A presentation of the results of a continuing interdisciplinary study of the potential applications of fixed and broadcast satellites for educational information transfer in the United States for the period 1975-1985.

Parker, Edwin B., and Dunn, D.A. "Information Technology: Its Social Potential." *Science.* Vol. 176, June 1972, pp. 1,392-1,399.

Support for the idea of financing pilot projects and coordinated planning that will test the technical and social feasibility of a *national* communications network providing access to a large number of retrieval systems in which nearly all information, entertainment, news, library archives and educational programs are available at any time to any person wanting them.

Parkus, Lawrence. "Computer-Assisted Instruction in Elementary/Secondary Education: The State of the Art," in Sidney G. Tickton, ed., *To Improve Learning: An Evaluation of Instructional Technology,* Vol. I. New York: Bowker, 1970, pp. 323-337.

Identification and review of several in-school CAI programs in terms of types, acceptability and results. Presentation of statistical research on effectiveness of the systems as well as their costs.

Pettit, Joseph M., and Grace, Donald J. "The Stanford Instructional Television Network." *IEEE Spectrum.* May 1970, pp. 73-80.

A description of the ITFS System employed by Stanford University to transmit continuing education programs in engineering to on-the-job graduate students at 25 different locations.

Polcyn, Kenneth A. "Current Communication Satellite Educational Experimentation: An Overview." *Audio-visual Instruction.* February 1973.

A brief overview of three educational experiments in Hawaii and between Stanford, California, and Brazil using Applications Technology Satellites.

The Videocassette and CATV Newsletter. "Microcampus—An Exclusive Report." February 1973.

A description of a system whereby courses at the University of Arizona are video-taped and then sent to students across the country for use at their own convenience. Includes the procedures, requirements and credits for on and off-campus courses.

Washington State University. "A Study of a Proposed Multi-purpose Communications System." July 1971.

An investigation of the feasibility of establishing a two-way television network in the southeastern Washington area for participants in continuing education studies and for certain graduate students.

Winslow, Ken. "The Adoption and Distribution of Videotape Materials for Educational Use," in Sidney G. Tickton, ed., *To Improve Learning; An Evaluation of Instructional Technology,* Vol. I. New York: Bowker, 1970, pp. 395-432.

A discussion of the software problem in educational television. Description of the adoption of videotape technology in education and the development of national or regional programming libraries.

International Perspectives

De Vera, Jose Maria. *Educational Television in Japan—Sophia University, Tokyo.* Rutland, Vermont: Tuttle, 1967.

An examination of the overall approach and effect of Japanese educational television, with an eye toward further collaboration between United States and Japanese broadcasters.

Groombridge, Brian, *et al. Adult Education and Television: A Comparative Study in Canada, Czechoslovakia and Japan.* Paris: UNESCO, September 1966.

A study of the educational uses and potential of television in three countries. Discusses the social and educational context, the kinds of programs and their purposes and the adult uses of educational television.

Kyratonis, Dorothee, and Vonhoff, Renate, eds. *Multi-media Systems in Adult Education; Twelve Project Descriptions in Nine Countries.* Munich: International Central Institute for Youth and Educational Television, 1972.

A description of 12 multi-media adult education projects in nine countries, including England, Japan, the Netherlands, West Germany, France, Poland and the United States. The first section of the book outlines eight steps for building an efficient out-of-school instructional media project.

Scupham, John. *The Open University.* London: International Broadcast Institute, 1972.

See Abstracts, pp. 162-167.

Scupham, John. *Broadcasting and the Community.* London: Watts, 1967.

An eloquent description of the programming of the BBC and the philosophy which underlies it. Emphasizes that the use of broadcasting for strictly educational purposes must be thought of as an important part of the educational strategy and culture transmission of every nation.

Siepmann, Charles E. "New Dimensions in British Higher Education: The Open University." *Educational Television.* November 1970.

Silleck, John. "Britain's Bold New Electronic University." *World.* December 5, 1972, pp. 28-32.

The latest update on the Open University, which uses 300 study centers, radio, TV and the mails to service 32,000 students.

Telecommunications Journal. "Japan: Full Schooling Provided by Cable Television." Vol. 40, April 1973, p. 189.

A short description of a four-channel cable system linking all schools in the town of Tateyama, Japan.

UNESCO. *Radio and Television in the Service of Education and Development in Asia.* Paris: UNESCO Reports and Papers on Mass Communication, No. 49, 1967.

Suggestions for the use of broadcasting to raise levels of health, formal and non-formal education, productivity, income, motivation, and national involvement of people in the developing countries of Asia.

Bibliographies and Guides

Cable Television Information Center. *Bibliocable.* Washington, D.C., April 1973.

A useful up-to-date guide to the basic literature on cable television.

Dale, Edgar, and Balland, John. *A Guide to the Literature on Audio-visual Instruction.* ERIC Clearinghouse on Media and Technology, Ohio State University, September 1971.

ERIC Clearinghouse on Adult Education. *Higher Education, No. 1 — Current information Sources.* Syracuse University, October 1967.

Information Center on Instructional Technology. *Sources of Information and Assistance on Educational Technology for Development: A Directory.* Washington, D.C.: Academy for Educational Development, July 1972.

Information on sources for training, software, hardware, professional and trade associations and financial assistance.

Le Duc, Don R. "A Selective Bibliography on the Evolution of CATV, 1950-1970." *Journal of Broadcasting.* Vol. XV, Spring 1971, pp. 195-234.

Molenda, Michael. *Annotated Bibliography of the Educational Implications of Cable Television.* School of Education, Indiana University, March 1973.

Molenda, Michael. "The Educational Implications of Cable Television and Video Cassettes: An Annotated Bibliography." *Audio-visual Instruction.* April 1972, pp. 42-59.

An emphasis on articles related to the CATV industry and its regulation.

Ohliger, John. *The Mass Media in Adult Education: A Review of Recent Literature.* ERIC Clearinghouse on Adult Education, Syracuse University, 1968.

Office of External Study Programs. *External Study for Post-Secondary Students — An Annotated Bibliography.* New York: CEEB, n.d. (Supplement, August 1972.)

Shafer, Jon. *Education and Cable Television—A Guide to Franchising and Utilization.* ERIC Clearinghouse on Media and Technology, Stanford University, January 1973.

Television and Film in College English Instructions: A Bibliography of Research and Studies with Abstracts. October 1969.

INDEX

The Aspen Program on Communications and Society, a joint program of the Aspen Institute for Humanistic Studies and the Academy for Educational Development, is being supported by grants from the Markle, Benton, Russell Sage, Irving B. Harris, Marcus and Harryette Cohn and Ford Foundations, as well as the National Endowment for the Humanities and the National Home Library Foundation.

ABOUT THE AUTHORS

Richard Adler

Mr. Adler, who is Associate Director of the Aspen Workshop on Uses of the Cable, previously served as assistant professor of English at Oberlin College and, before that, as an instructor in English at the University of California, Berkeley. He holds an undergraduate degree, *magna cum laude,* from Harvard and did his graduate work in English at Berkeley.

His interest in cable television arises from his experiences as the initiator and instructor of the first video production course at Oberlin. Subsequently, he was appointed chairman of a presidential committee on cable television at Oberlin, wrote a report describing potential uses of cable by the college, and was a member of the Oberlin City Council Commission on Cable Television.

Walter S. Baer

Dr. Baer is a graduate of the California Institute of Technology and holds a Ph.D. in physics from the University of Wisconsin. After serving as a member of the technical staff at Bell Telephone Laboratories, he was selected in a national competition as a White House Fellow and worked during 1966-67 in the office of Vice President Humphrey. He later served on the White House science advisory staff and, as an independent consultant, worked with the United Nations in analyzing its communications systems.

Dr. Baer currently is Director of the Aspen Workshop on Uses of the Cable. He also is a consultant to the Communications Policy Program of The Rand Corporation, where he has directed technical and economic studies of cable television. His Rand publications include: *Interactive Television: Prospects for Two-Way Services on Cable* (1971); *Cable Television: A Handbook for Decision-making* (1973); and *Cable Television: A Guide to the Technology* (with Carl Pilnick, 1973).

RELATED TITLES
Published by Praeger Special Studies

ASPEN NOTEBOOK ON GOVERNMENT
AND THE MEDIA

edited by William L. Rivers and Michael J. Nyhan

CABLE TELEVISION U.S.A.
An Analysis of Government Policy

Martin H. Seiden

TELEVISION PROGRAMMING FOR NEWS
AND PUBLIC AFFAIRS
A Quantitative Analysis of Networks and Stations

Frank Wolf

MASS MEDIA AND THE ENVIRONMENT
Water Resources, Land Use, and Atomic Energy in California

David M. Rubin and David P. Sachs

CHILDREN AND THE URBAN ENVIRONMENT:
A LEARNING EXPERIENCE
Evaluation of the WGBH-TV Educational Project

prepared by Marshall Kaplan, Gans, and Kahn

CHILDREN'S TELEVISION COMMERCIALS
A Content Analysis

Charles Winick, Lorne G. Williamson, Stuart F. Chuzmir,
and Mariann Pezzella Winick